Ethics Case Studies for Health Information Management

Ethics Case Studies for Health Information Management

Leah A. Grebner MS, RHIA, CCS

DELMAR
CENGAGE Learning·

Australia · Brazil · Japan · Korea · Mexico · Singapore · Spain · United Kingdom · United States

Ethics Case Studies for Health Information Management

Leah A. Grebner, MS, RHIA, CCS, FAHIMA

Vice President, Career and Professional
  Editorial: Dave Garza

Director of Learning Solutions: Matthew Kane

Senior Acquisitions Editor: Rhonda Dearborn

Managing Editor: Marah Bellegarde

Editorial Assistant: Chiara Astriab

Vice President, Career and Professional
  Marketing: Jennifer McAvey

Marketing Director: Wendy Mapstone

Marketing Director: Michele McTighe

Production Director: Carolyn Miller

Content Project Manager: Brooke Greenhouse

Senior Art Director: Jack Pendleton

For product information and technology assistance, contact us at
Professional & Career Group Customer Support, 1-800-648-7450
For permission to use material from this text or product,
submit all requests online at **cengage.com/permissions**.
Further permissions questions can be e-mailed to
permissionrequest@cengage.com.

Library of Congress Control Number: 2008931914

ISBN-13: 978-1418049300
ISBN-10: 1418049301

Delmar
5 Maxwell Drive
Clifton Park, NY 12065-2919
USA

Cengage Learning products are represented in Canada
by Nelson Education, Ltd.

For your lifelong learning solutions, visit **delmar.cengage.com**
Visit our corporate website at **cengage.com.**

Notice to the Reader

Publisher does not warrant or guarantee any of the products described herein or perform any independent analysis in connection with any of the product information contained herein. Publisher does not assume, and expressly disclaims, any obligation to obtain and include information other than that provided to it by the manufacturer. The reader is expressly warned to consider and adopt all safety precautions that might be indicated by the activities described herein and to avoid all potential hazards. By following the instructions contained herein, the reader willingly assumes all risks in connection with such instructions. The publisher makes no representations or warranties of any kind, including but not limited to, the warranties of fitness for particular purpose or merchantability, nor are any such representations implied with respect to the material set forth herein, and the publisher takes no responsibility with respect to such material. The publisher shall not be liable for any special, consequential, or exemplary damages resulting, in whole or part, from the readers' use of, or reliance upon, this material.

Printed in United States
1 2 3 4 5 XX 10 09 08

Contents

Preface

We are all familiar with the ever-changing environment with evolving technology and regulatory guidelines faced by today's health information professionals. This dynamic health care arena requires those employed in all aspects of the health information field to continuously keep abreast of ethical issues related to technology and legal issues to appropriately and ethically manage some of the obstacles we face in our daily routines. The intent of this case study book is to provide exposure to a cross-section of the many ethical dilemmas faced by this generation's health information professionals.

Organization of Book

The introductory chapter explains the author's case study methodology that teaches the reader to outline ethical problems along with potential solutions with the ultimate goal of choosing the best possible solution.

Each of the 30 cases opens with a brief scenario and ends with a series of questions that guide the reader through a critical thinking thought process that enables the reader to make the best decision. Additionally, the book contains a correlation grid that maps the case topics to American Health Information Management Association Credential Use and Scope of Practice.

Also available for the instructor is the *Instructors Manual to Accompany Ethics Case Studies for Health Information Management*, ISBN 10: 1-4180-4931-X/ISBN 13: 978-1-4180-4831-7. The Instructors Manual contains suggested solutions to the case studies and ideas on how to incorporate the use of case studies into your curriculum.

Author Acknowledgements

The author would like to thank the reviewers of this edition for their valuable feedback:

Cathy Kelly-Arney, CMA, RMA, MLTC, BSHS
Institutional Director of Healthcare Education
National College and National College of Business and Technology
100 Logan Street
Bluefield VA 24605

Patrice Jackson, RHIT, CHP, CCS
Health Information Instructor
Heald College
Mililani, HI

Debra Long, MS, RHIA, RHIT, CCS
Lamar Institute of Technology
Program Director
Beaumont, TX

Patricia Shaw, MEd, RHIA, FAHIMA
Associate Professor and Program Director
Weber State University
Ogden, UT

There have been many health information professionals who have influenced me in my career in a variety of ways, but there are three who have affected me the strongest. I would like to extend a sincere thank you to Janet Bertschy, who hired me in my first entry level medical records position as I was pursuing education in a clinical health care field, and Mary Sierra, who introduced me to the wonderful world of health information when I discovered that hands-on patient care was not my career of choice. I would also like to thank Bonnie Murphy and Maggie Starr, who have been instrumental as mentors as I have developed my career as an educator in the health information field. Without their encouragement and words of wisdom and support, I do not feel I would have chosen this path in my career. There was a point in my teaching career that I was discouraged about the lack of a good text for one of the subjects I taught. One of my mentors commented to me, "Why don't you just write your own book?" At the time, I did not take the comment seriously, but as more time passed, I found myself frequently returning to that thought, and the thought developed into a dream. Of course, I could not neglect thanking my family for their moral support and proofreading as I have pursued this project. Finally, I thank you, the reader, as you experience my dream becoming a reality through this publication. Enjoy!

Correlation of Case Studies to the American Health Information Management Association (AHIMA) Credential List and Scope of Practice

Chapter Title	AHIMA Credential Use and Scope of Practice	Joint Commission on Accreditation of Healthcare Organizations	Occupational Safety and Health Administration	Incident Reports	Human Resource Management	Noncompete Clause	Access to Information	Release of Information	Minor Patient	Health Insurance Portability and Accountability Act (HIPAA) Privacy	Confidentiality	Mental Health Treatment Records	HIPAA Security	Electronic Health Record	Drug and Alcohol Treatment Records	Human Immunodeficiency Virus/Acquired Immune Deficiency Syndrome	Centers for Medicare and Medicaid Services Guidelines	Coding/Billing/Reimbursement	Compliance	Documentation	Malpractice	Mandated Reporting	Stark Laws
CASE 1 But I Consider Myself to be Credentialed	X																						
CASE 2 Scope of Practice	X																						
CASE 3 To Suspend or Not to Suspend?		X	X																				
CASE 4 Difficulty with Doctors				X																			
CASE 5 Incidental Finding																							
CASE 6 Divided Loyalty					X	X																	
CASE 7 The Case of the Missing Record							X																
CASE 8 Which comes First, the Patient or.....							X											X					
CASE 9 Physician Access to Information as a Noncustodial Parent							X	X	X														
CASE 10 International Release of Information I								X															
CASE 11 International Release of Information II								X															
CASE 12 Compliance Matters								X									X	X	X				X

CASE 13 Will the Real Expert Please Stand up?								X		X													
CASE 14 A Minor Confidentiality Issue									X	X												X	
CASE 15 Final Lesson before Graduation										X	X												
CASE 16 Internal Confidentiality Matters										X								X					
CASE 17 The Public Needs to Know... Don't They?										X					X								
CASE 18 Protecting a Friend										X						X							
CASE 19 What Next?										X	X	X											
CASE 20 On the Floor										X													
CASE 21 Protection of Passwords													X										
CASE 22 Electronic Health Record Security													X	X									
CASE 23 A "Free" Gift													X	X									
CASE 24 Two Halves Do Not Always Make a Whole																							
CASE 25 If It Was Documented, Was It Done?																		X					
CASE 26 Who's the Coder?																		X		X			
CASE 27 New Kid on the Block																		X	X	X			
CASE 28 Legibility and Timeliness Go Hand-In-Hand																		X	X	X			
CASE 29 A Case That Hits Close to Home																				X	X		
APPENDIX 1 American Health Information Management Association Code of Ethics																							

Introduction and Explanation of Case Study Methodology

The case study method is a useful tool for exploring all aspects of a case that is presented for evaluation. This method allows the evaluator to outline problems in the case along with potential solutions. The potential solutions are then outlined with the pros and cons of each. The evaluator then determines the best possible solution and provides additional details, including logistics and timeline of implementation.

The case study method is something that can be applied to any field of practice. It is a tool that will benefit the user by providing a more comprehensive evaluation of a problem. The case study method prompts the user to explore all possible solutions, addressing positive and negative aspects to provide a higher level of analysis. This more in-depth look at the problem will allow the user to select the solution that is more likely to be the best for the identified problem in the particular situation. It allows the user to customize the problem-solving process to a specific situation, rather than simply implementing a canned band-aid solution that may not be appropriate for the setting or circumstances.

The following is a simple example utilization of the case study method. Mary is the director of Health Information Services in a small hospital. She has two coders, Sally and Jane, who have been on staff for greater than 10 years, are both highly productive, and consistently demonstrate accuracy of 99% or better on quality audits. Jane had an emergency room visit, during which it was determined she was human immunodeficiency virus (HIV)-positive. Sally coded the record and told the other staff members that they should be careful around Jane because of her HIV status. Jane found out about Sally's distribution of her HIV status to the department and has decided to pursue legal action against the facility for not appropriately maintaining confidentiality of her information. Using the case study method, evaluate possible actions that should be taken and determine the best option.

Case Study Evaluation of Problem

Problem: Sally has violated confidentiality of HIV status.

Solution One: Mary should give Sally a verbal warning and make her apologize to Jane. Her intentions were probably simply to protect her coworkers.

Pros:

1. This solution would prevent the need to find a replacement coder.

Cons:

1. There is a pending legal action against the facility regarding dissemination of HIV status involving Sally's actions.
2. Sally's actions violate laws regarding confidentiality of HIV status.

Solution Two: Mary should terminate Sally.

Pros:

1. This solution will prevent a repeat episode of breach of confidentiality by Sally.
2. Terminating Sally would be in the best interest of the facility considering the pending legal action.

Cons:
1. Mary will lose half of her coding manpower and have to find a replacement coder.
2. Sally's intentions were probably innocent and what she felt was in the best interest of her coworkers.

Proposed Solution: Mary should terminate Sally.

Implementation Plan: Mary will meet with the Director of Human Resources to ensure the termination is handled appropriately, and she will follow established organizational guidelines for the situation.

The case study method is something that you can use in any aspect of your life or career. Maybe you are trying to make a decision about moving out of state, changing jobs, getting married, or starting a family. Simply utilize the case method to outline all of the variables in your decision to narrow down to the best possible solution. The possibilities are endless for how you can apply the case study method in your life.

But I Consider Myself to Be Credentialed

Lydia graduated at the top of her class from Anystate University. Following graduation, she started her career as a coder, in what was then known as Medical Records at Rosewood General Hospital. She successfully passed the Registered Records Administrator exam and, in a few years, was promoted to the position of Assistant Director of Medical Records. Later that year, Lydia met Theodore, and they were married the following year. Lydia continued in her position as Assistant Director of Medical Records at Rosewood for three more years until Theodore was transferred to a position in another state. Lydia resigned her position and relocated with Theodore and their two-year-old daughter.

Lydia had no trouble finding employment after the move. She accepted a position as Lead Coder at Greenlawn Hospital. While working at this facility, Lydia appreciated significant professional growth; she was promoted to Assistant Director and, eventually, Interim Director of Medical Records at Greenlawn. During her term as Interim Director of Medical Records, the American Medical Records Association changed to the American Health Information Management Association (AHIMA). Lydia took steps to change the name of the Medical Records department at Greenlawn to Health Information Services. Lydia also delivered twins during her time serving as Director at Greenlawn.

The Health Information Management career field underwent numerous changes, and Lydia attended continuing education seminars to ensure she was up-to-date in her knowledge of the dynamic rules and regulations related to PPS, the Health Insurance Portability and Accountability Act, corporate compliance, and other new issues that popped up along the way. Administration at Greenlawn Hospital eventually offered Lydia the position of becoming the permanent Director of Health Information Services, which she gladly accepted. However, during this very busy time in her life, between her growing family and keeping up with her career, Lydia failed to keep up her credentials through AHIMA. At one point, Lydia made a point of investigating what she would need to do to get her credentials reinstated, but this reinstatement was certainly not a priority in her life at the time.

Lydia kept in close contact with her classmates from Anystate University, which soon proved to be beneficial to her. Theodore was transferred once again, meaning another relocation for the family. Luckily, one of Lydia's close friends from school, Fernando, was Director of Health Information Management at Springfield Memorial Hospital, and he was looking for a Coding Manager. As soon as Fernando received news of Lydia moving to his area, he told her about the position and said that it would be hers if she was interested. Back in their college days, Lydia frequently tutored Fernando in coding, so he was confident enough of her abilities that he did not require her to take a coding test prior to employment. Fernando also knew about Lydia's continuous employment in the Health Information Management field and that she consistently attended continuing education seminars, so the thought of verifying her credentials did not cross his mind because Springfield Memorial Hospital did not require their coders to hold credentials.

Lydia continued to work at Springfield Memorial, and prior to a Joint Commission survey, the issue of her lapsed credentials surfaced. She discussed the process of reinstatement through AHIMA with Fernando, but because it was not required for her position, it was not addressed as an urgent issue. Lydia had become busy outside of work dealing with her children, who had become teenagers, and divorcing Theodore, who had left her for another woman.

Lydia looked for additional part-time work to pay her growing list of monthly bills. She taught medical terminology at a local community college. Another of her old college friends, Matilda, was director of a Commission on

Accreditation for Health Informatics and Information Management (CAHIIM)-accredited Health Information Management program at another local college. Matilda was in desperate need of additional adjunct faculty and had talked to Lydia over lunch one day about the possibility of teaching nights. Lydia really needed additional money, so she eagerly accepted the position. Matilda, like Fernando, was aware of Lydia's career achievements and her frequent attendance of continuing education activities. Matilda hired Lydia, whose resume indicated she held the Registered Health Information Administrator (RHIA) credential.

The following semester, Matilda started gathering data for an upcoming CAHIIM site survey and had requested the required information related to her faculty members' continuing education activities. Lydia provided Matilda with copies of certificates to provide appropriate evidence of her attendance at seminars, which provided significantly more than the required number of continuing education credits for maintenance of the RHIA credential. Matilda also requested a copy of Lydia's RHIA certificate. However, Lydia explained that most of her professional documents were still packed in boxes from her move back to the state, plus she was also in the process of packing her belongings to put the house that she owned with Theodore up for sale. Matilda accepted the excuse and figured the document really was not that important to the CAHIIM surveyors because they could easily obtain the document from AHIMA if necessary.

The CAHIIM surveyors arrived, did their preliminary review of data, met with Matilda, and then met with the students and individual instructors. During her meeting with the surveyors, Matilda could not say enough about how Lydia was one of her best instructors, and they were impressed at the experience she had to share with the students. The surveyors received equally positive comments about Lydia from the students they interviewed.

At the end of the site survey, Matilda met with the survey team and was astounded to learn from them that Lydia did not hold any AHIMA credentials. They did reinforce the fact that her extensive experience, especially in the coding arena, qualified her to teach medical terminology and coding. However, the surveyors explained that Lydia would not be qualified to teach any other courses specific to health information management until she successfully had her credentials reinstated through AHIMA, which she indicated to the surveyors that she was completely willing to do. The surveyors explained to Matilda that because Lydia was qualified to teach some of the courses, they would not officially document the issue, but they wanted to make her aware of the situation.

Discussion Questions

1. Should Matilda or Fernando have been aware of Lydia's credential status?

2. Should Matilda inform her organization's administration of Lydia's credential status? Why or why not?

3. Matilda and Fernando are close friends. Matilda suspects that Fernando may not be aware of Lydia's credential status. Should she alert him of the issue as a colleague? Why or why not?

4. How should Matilda respond to Lydia following the survey?

5. What legal and ethical issues are addressed in this case?

6. Using the case method, evaluate possible actions that should be taken and determine the best option.

CASE 2

Scope of Practice

Nadia is a registered health information technician who works as a release of information specialist at Anytown General Hospital. Prior to going to school for Health Information Technology, she had completed a year and a half of nursing school. She maintained a 4.00 grade point average in nursing school and did well in her classes. However, she decided that she did not care for the hands-on patient care aspect of health care. Nadia especially liked her pathophysiology and pharmacology courses when she was in school and had been considering going back to school to prepare for a clinical research position.

Nadia always received excellent performance evaluations from her supervisor. She consistently did well at all aspects of her position and was always willing to offer additional help for others in the department. She frequently answered disease process questions for the coders because they appreciated her knowledge and experience from nursing school.

One day, a patient and his wife presented to the release of information area to pick up a copy of the patient's recent test results to take to a specialist. The patient asked Nadia for some assistance in reading the report because he was unsure of the terminology. Nadia was thrilled to help the patient. The patient had bilateral Doppler studies done on his legs to follow up from a deep venous thrombosis (DVT). Nadia was not terribly familiar with the format of the results, but she did not want the patient or her peers to know that she was not 100% sure of her interpretation. She did not see anything that looked alarming (to her), so she told the patient and his wife that as far as she could tell, everything looked normal.

The patient was an avid runner and had been on bedrest since being diagnosed with the DVT. He did not have an appointment to see the vascular specialist until next week. He and his wife discussed the fact that the woman who gave them the test results interpreted them as normal and that it should be safe for him to get out and run again. The patient and his wife went out for what they planned to be a three-mile run. However, two miles into the run, the patient developed severe chest pain and shortness of breath and collapsed. His wife called for help, and he was taken to the Anytown General emergency room (ER). Soon after arrival, he was pronounced expired due to an embolism. The ER physician discussed what happened with the patient's wife and explained that he had reviewed the Doppler study they had picked up, and it clearly demonstrated that the DVT was still present. He explained that when the patient was running, the clot became mobile and migrated to the pulmonary artery. The patient's wife explained to the ER physician that the woman who provided copies of their records interpreted the results for them and told them that the tests appeared normal. The physician explained that the person who gave them the records was not properly trained or licensed to determine diagnosis or interpret test results and that they should have waited for the specialist to review the tests.

Discussion Questions

1. What could the implications of the release of the information clerk's actions be for the facility?

2. What could the implications of the release of information clerk's actions be for herself?

3. What could have been done differently?

4. What internal and external forces impact this case?

5. What are the legal issues addressed in this case?

6. What are the ethical issues addressed in this case?

7. How are the ethical issues in this case covered in the American Health Information Management Association Code of Ethics?

8. Using the case method, evaluate possible actions that should be taken and determine the best option.

CASE 3

To Suspend or Not to Suspend?

Maya works at Community Medical Center as Assistant Director of the Health Information Services department. She has worked in Health Information Management for the past 15 years, although she is new to this facility within the past two weeks. Maya is aware of statistics that must be maintained for the Joint Commission and for licensing purposes. Her previous work experience has included Physician Record Assistant at a 250-bed acute care hospital and Director of Health Information Services at a large Joint Commission-accredited acute care facility with an associated skilled nursing facility and a level I trauma center.

Suspension of physicians for incomplete records is done each Wednesday at the Community Medical Center. The first Wednesday that Maya is observing D'Shondra, the Physician Record Assistant, compiling the statistics and list of physicians who are to be suspended, she notices that there are six physicians who have incomplete records and should be suspended. Maya alerts D'Shondra to the fact that she had neglected to include these six physicians on the suspension list and the statistical data for suspension and delinquency rates. D'Shondra responds by explaining to Maya that there is an unwritten rule that these physicians are not to be suspended under any circumstances. When Maya questioned the rationale for failure to suspend this select group of physicians, D'Shondra tells her, "It's been this organization's unwritten policy ever since I've been here. I just follow directions and accept the fact that there is probably a good reason for it."

Maya is concerned not only about the fairness to the rest of the physicians on staff but also regarding the accuracy of statistics that are compiled each week and integrity of documentation. She takes her concerns to Barbara, the Director of Health Information Services. Barbara explains to Maya that there are a variety of reasons behind the apparent noncompliant suspension process. One of the physicians brings a significant number of patients to the facility and has a history of threatening to take his patients to the competing hospital across town if he is ever suspended by Community Medical Center due to incomplete records. Two of the other physicians are cardiac surgeons who have stated to administration that if they are ever suspended due to delinquent records, they will no longer utilize the facility for their surgical cases. Community Medical Center went through a difficult process to entice the cardiac surgeons to refer their cases to the open heart surgical unit just five years ago, when the unit was added. Part of the negotiation process with these physicians included a gentleman's agreement with the medical center's administration that they would not be suspended for delinquent records.

Barbara explained that the fourth physician who was not included for suspension is the brother-in-law of Community Medical Center's Chief Executive Officer. This physician did not have a history of threatening to take his business elsewhere; rather, he had simply taken advantage of his family ties with the Chief Executive Officer to gain a grace period for completing his records for the sake of convenience.

The final two physicians who had been left from the list, Barbara explained, are simply handled with kid gloves because they tend to be general nuisances to the organization if things are not done their own way. One of them is a general surgeon who does the majority of his procedures at Community Medical Center because he and his patients prefer the facility. However, this physician has poor organizational and prioritizing skills and rarely completes his records without a significant amount of reminders from the Physician Record Assistant. He has been able to convince the Chief Executive Officer that the competing hospital across town has made him exempt from suspension, and he has an agreement that he will complete his records as soon as possible each month as long as he is exempt from suspension. Dr. McDonald is an older physician who has been on staff at Community

Medical Center for the past 30 years and was supposedly grandfathered into being exempt from the suspension process many years ago. He is only on staff at Community Medical Center and not at the other facility. He has a history of creating a scene when previous Physician Record Assistants have tried to suspend him for incomplete records, then taking his complaint about suspension to administration, where the ruling to suspend is revoked.

Maya prides herself in meticulously adhering to laws, rules and regulations, and organizational bylaws. When working at previous facilities, she consistently ensured that the facilities' statistics were accurately reported. Because of her dedication to honesty in reporting statistics, she felt that it would be appropriate to take this issue to administration, assuming the senior administrators of the facility were equally as dedicated to calculating and reporting accurate statistics. Unfortunately, this did not seem to be the case when she presented the issue. The Chief Executive Officer reminded her that keeping the physicians happy should be priority because without these physicians being able to admit patients or schedule surgical procedures, the organization's revenue would decrease. He assured her that the current unwritten policy for these physicians being exempt from suspension of privileges has worked fine for years and that it would not be fiscally responsible to change now. He also reminded her of the importance of the confidential nature of the unwritten policy to prevent other physicians from expecting similar treatment.

Discussion Questions

1. What internal and external forces impact Maya's concerns in this case?

2. What ethical concerns are presented in this case?

3. Are there any legal issues that need to be considered regarding this case?

4. What additional questions or issues should Maya present to administration?

5. What options does Maya have if administration does not respond to her concerns?

6. If you were in this position, do you feel it would be worth the risk of losing your job to stand up to administration regarding the facility's unwritten physician suspension policy for delinquent records?

7. Using the case method, evaluate possible actions that Maya should take and determine the best option.

CASE 4

Difficulty with Doctors

St. John's Hospital is a 200-bed hospital in a city of 150,000 people. Most of the physicians have been on staff for greater than 15 years and are mainly older, well-established physicians and surgeons. The Health Information Services department enjoys a low turnover rate and has many long-term employees. The older physicians have had more experience with fee-for-service payment and still have difficulty adjusting to documentation requirements associated with prospective payment systems. They are also accustomed to an atmosphere where the physicians are highly respected and complete tasks on their own schedules. Some of the physicians are very demanding, which has become accepted practice at St. John's.

Elijah, the Physician Record Assistant, has been at St. John's for 30 years. She recently submitted her retirement notice, and her replacement, Katarina, was hired with two weeks to train with Elijah. Katarina went through the usual organizational and departmental orientation and then proceeded to training for her new position. Elijah started by showing her around the filing areas, dictation room, and other areas in the hospital where physicians complete their records. Once they returned to the department, Elijah showed Katarina how to run deficiency lists for physicians, reports for statistics, and the suspension process. So far, Katarina is happy with her new position at St. John's.

Dr. Chen was the first physician to come in for his records to be pulled during Katarina's training. Katarina was able to easily locate all of his records, and he thanked her when she was finished.

The next physician to come in was Dr. Jorge Hernandez, who has served five terms as Chief of Medical Staff, been on staff at St. John's for 30 years, and has established a high sense of respect from hospital staff at all levels. Dr. Hernandez is well-known by all employees at the hospital, and he expects immediate service when he makes demands. He approaches Katarina, stating abruptly, "I need my charts before my ten o'clock case." Katarina asks who he is, and Elijah tells her and also lets her know of his high expectations. She also fills her in that Dr. Hernandez always pushes his limits with delinquent records, only coming in when he has been called prior to having his privileges suspended. Katarina is able to find all of his charts except for one that is tagged on the report as a high-priority record for billing. Dr. Hernandez completes the rest of his records and Katarina informs him that there is still a high-priority record that he needs to complete. Dr. Hernandez tells Katarina that he is a busy surgeon, and he does not have time to wait around for one record. He leaves before she is able to respond. Katarina is upset that in her second encounter with a physician, she has failed to get a high-priority billing record completed and that it could be a couple of weeks before Dr. Hernandez returns to complete his records again. Katarina locates the record right after he leaves and contacts his office about whether or not there is a possibility of making arrangements to get the record taken to him elsewhere for completion. His receptionist informs her that he does his hospital records on his schedule and that he does not want to be bothered outside of that time.

Dr. Mark Stone's office calls next requesting his records to be pulled. Elijah alerts Katarina about his temper. Dr. Stone has built a reputation for throwing tantrums if his demands are not immediately met. Many hospital employees suspect that he is becoming senile. Dr. Stone has been rumored to have fits in the operating room, throwing scalpels and other sharp instruments. Katarina thinks that the information is exaggerated and does not worry too much. She pulls his records and is pleased that she locates all of them before he gets there after her experience with Dr. Hernandez. Dr. Stone comes in, Katarina directs him to where his records are, and things seem to go well until he finds a record marked as needing a dictated report that he thinks he has already completed. He hollers for somebody to help him, so Katarina goes to see what the problem is. She kindly tells him that she will check on the status of the report, which is not acceptable to him. He responds by throwing the chart at her, the corner hitting her directly in the eye, causing a corneal laceration and a laceration of the orbital area the ends up requiring sutures in the emergency department. Still worked up about his deficient record, he does not notice the injury he has caused to Katarina and the sudden attention the staff is giving her; rather, he continues into the Health Information Services department looking for a supervisor. While he is in the director's office, Sarah, the Health Information Services Director, is contacted by the emergency department staff to alert her of the incident.

Discussion Questions

1. What internal and external forces impact Elijah, Katarina, Sarah, and the physicians in this case?

2. What ethical concerns are presented in this case?

3. What legal issues need to be considered regarding this case?

4. How could Sarah and the hospital administrators respond to each issue presented?

5. Do you feel that Katarina acted appropriately?

6. What could have been done to prevent the incident yet ensure that the physician's records are completed in a timely manner?

7. What action(s) do you feel is appropriate to respond to the incident?

8. Using the case method, identify what you consider to be the greatest legal or ethical dilemma in this case and determine the best option for resolution.

CASE 5

Incidental Finding

Janet Lewis was a registered nurse at Hillside Community Hospital. She had been working numerous extra shifts to cover hours from vacant positions. On top of that, she was a single mother of a child with developmental disabilities, which frequently left her exhausted. Janet had no family to assist her, and she was new in town. Her work schedule did not allow time for socializing, so she had not yet established any close friends to help in times of need.

Saturday afternoon, Janet was looking forward to going home after working 72 hours that week; she had just three more hours until she could go to bed. Next thing she knew, two of the second shift nurses called sick, and Janet agreed to cover for one of them. The shift was relatively quiet and uneventful until one of Janet's patients was found unresponsive in his room: a code blue at the end of her shift. Janet normally reacted very well in these situations, but she was barely coherent from lack of sleep.

The patient had developed severe bradycardia. The physician attending the call requested atropine. Janet was having trouble focusing, so she asked the physician to clarify; again, atropine was requested. She grabbed a vial from the crash cart, inadvertently reading the label from the vial next to the one she grabbed: lidocaine. She drew up the ordered amount and handed it off to the doctor. The patient's condition worsened. The physician demanded more atropine. Janet was still holding the lidocaine vial and proceeded to dispense the ordered amount. Janet replaced the vial on the crash cart, when the physician ordered additional atropine. She grabbed the vial labeled as atropine and dispensed to the physician. It was at this point that Janet realized she possibly had the wrong medication previously. However, in the hectic moment of the code, she hesitated to inform the physician. After additional resuscitative measures were attempted, the code was called, and the patient was pronounced expired.

The physician spoke with the family immediately after the code, and then they went into the room to view the expired patient. Janet approached the physician when he returned to the nurses' station to complete his documentation. She explained that she possibly gave him the incorrect medication. An incident report was completed, and in the rush, it was filed on the chart instead of being sent to Risk Management. What Janet and the physician did not know was that a member of the patient's family, who was leaving, overheard the conversation but did not address it with Janet or the physician.

Carla was new to the health information management field and was working in her first "real" job at Hillside Community Hospital as an Assembly and Analysis Clerk. She had been in her position for six months and was competent in her work. She occasionally encountered unfamiliar documents and generally asked questions when she found forms that could not determine where to file. Carla worked second shift on Sunday night when she got to the chart with Janet's incident report. She was the only person covering the office on Sunday evenings. When Carla stumbled on the incident report and did not have anybody to ask about it, she simply filed it behind the miscellaneous tab because her trainer failed to mention anything about sending incident reports to Risk Management.

The following week, the patient's family contacted an attorney and presented the hospital with a malpractice lawsuit. A subpoena was sent for copies of the record. The Release of Information Specialist had an unexpected family medical emergency, so others in the department were covering the position. Carla had volunteered to work extra hours and was helping prepare records for release of information. Still unaware that incident reports were not to be part of the medical record, Carla included Janet's incident report in the copies, and they were delivered.

Jose, the Director of Health Information Services, was on vacation during this time. Because Hillside Community Hospital had a small Health Information Services department, there were not any Assistant Director or supervisors. The subpoena required that copies of the records be delivered in person to the Hillside courthouse, so Jose had Carla take them.

Discussion Questions

1. Identify actions that could have been taken by each individual, who could have reduced the risk for Hillside Community Hospital.

2. What internal and external forces impact this case?

3. What are the legal issues addressed in this case?

4. What are the ethical issues addressed in this case?

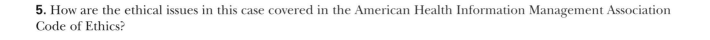
5. How are the ethical issues in this case covered in the American Health Information Management Association Code of Ethics?

6. Using the case method, evaluate possible actions that should be taken and determine the best option.

CASE 6

Divided Loyalty

Ahmed was working for 300.01 Coding, a national coding consulting company, as Manager of Traveling Coding and New Accounts. He had been with 300.01 Coding as a traveling coder for 10 years prior to his promotion to management. Ahmed, a true expert in his field, was well-versed in coding in any type of care setting, and he knew the regulations inside and out. He had developed an extensive network in the health information management field. Ahmed's professional accomplishments included several journal publications and numerous presentations at regional, state, and national educational meetings.

Ahmed's duties related to new accounts included contacting facilities that had never contracted with 300.01 Coding in the past and those that had, but not for the past year. Today, Ahmed was working on a list of previous clients. He recalled 300.01 Coding developing an excellent rapport with Springfield General Hospital when he was working as a traveling coder.

Ahmed had gone on an assignment at Springfield General Hospital five years ago. He worked there for a year and a half and became close with the coding staff and the director. They all developed great respect for Ahmed's coding abilities, speed and accuracy of his work, and extensive knowledge of coding guidelines and regulations. Jessica, the Director of Health Information Services at Springfield General, wished she could hire Ahmed at that time, but she was prohibited from doing so because of a noncompete clause in the contract between Springfield General and 300.01 Coding (see sample noncompete clause in box below). Jessica had kept in touch with Ahmed over the five-year period because they attended many of the same educational conferences.

Ahmed's timing for his call to Springfield General was perfect. Jessica had just received notice that one of her coders would be going on maternity leave earlier than anticipated because of pregnancy complications. Jessica congratulated Ahmed on his promotion to management and asked if there was any way that Springfield General would be able to convince him to go on the assignment at their facility, should they initiate a new contract with 300.01 Coding. Ahmed told her that he would check into it and get back to her. Ahmed discussed the assignment with the Chief Operating Officer of 300.01, who approved. The contract was signed, and Ahmed was off to Springfield at the start of the following week.

When Ahmed arrived, he was reoriented to the department and coding area. He was familiar with the encoder, abstracting software, chart order, and forms used at Springfield General, making it easy for him to start coding with no training time delay. Ahmed was exceeding the productivity standards of the contract between 300.01 Coding and Springfield General with exceptional accuracy. Jessica and the rest of the coding staff were thrilled to have him back at Springfield. Ahmed enjoyed working at Springfield General and loved the working conditions. He occasionally socialized with the coding staff and Jessica after working hours.

A month into Ahmed's coding assignment at Springfield General, Jessica called him into her office. She explained to him that she had just received a notice of resignation from one of the coders who would have to move out of state because of her husband's job being transferred. Ahmed assumed that this simply meant that his on-site assignment would be extended, meaning a greater commission for him because he landed the account. Unfortunately, what Jessica presented to Ahmed next was not that simple.

Jessica informed Ahmed that she had discussed the situation with the Chief Financial Officer (CFO) and Chief Executive Officer (CEO) of Springfield General Hospital. Jessica pointed out to the CFO and the CEO that there was a significant decrease in accounts receivable days since Ahmed had been there and convinced them that it would be beneficial to the organization to hire Ahmed as a coder. Ahmed reminded Jessica of the noncompete clause in the contract between Springfield General and 300.01 Coding. She stated that they had already taken that into consideration, and the organization would be willing to pay the penalty fee for breaking that clause because the difference of having Ahmed as a permanent member of their coding team would make up for it in a short amount of time. His next response was that he, too, had a noncompete clause in his contract with 300.01 Coding that prohibited him from working for a current, prospective, or past client within three years of termination of his contract with the company. Ahmed was also aware that 300.01 took this noncompete clause very seriously because they had previously taken legal action against another employee who had broken the clause after termination in the past year.

Jessica stated that she understood Ahmed's predicament but that she would like him to consider her offer. Jessica presented him with a highly competitive pay rate and benefits offer, along with a $10,000 sign-on bonus plus paying 100% of any moving expenses. The pay rate that Jessica presented to Ahmed was $10,000 more per year than his current salary. On top of that, he would be an hourly employee, eligible for overtime, and he would no longer have to deal with the hassles of management. He would be working Monday through Friday without worrying about getting calls from staff members working on weekends as he did in his position at 300.01 Coding.

Ahmed explained to Jessica that he would have to consider her offer and that he would get back to her the next day. This offer seemed too good to be true for him, but he could not help but think about the ordeal that 300.01 Coding was still creating for the previous employee who broke the noncompete clause. Ahmed did not know how to handle this dilemma.

Sample of Noncompete Clause

Furthermore, during the period of your employment, and for a period of (2) years thereafter, you hereby agree that you will not directly or indirectly engage in competition in any way with the Company by being associated with any consulting business or other business that may compete with the Company in any area that the Company may be engaged in business or any area for which the Company has submitted proposals for business. The term "competition" as used in the foregoing shall include, but not be limited to, attempts to divert clients, employees, subcontractors, or accounts from the Company and attempts to induce employees of the Company to terminate their employment. You hereby agree that "Your Organization" shall be entitled to enforce the provisions of this contract by any legal means. Such means shall include that right to enjoin you by legal process from violating the provisions hereof.

Discussion Questions

1. What internal and external forces impact this case?

2. What are the legal issues addressed in this case?

3. What are the ethical issues addressed in this case?

4. Are there any areas in this case that are addressed by the American Health Information Management Association Code of Ethics?

5. Does your state recognize noncompete clauses in contracts?

6. What questions does Ahmed need to address as he makes his decision?

7. Using the case method, evaluate possible actions that should be taken and determine the best option.

CASE 7

The Case of the Missing Record

Helene Maxwell was a 65-year-old woman who lived alone. Her husband had passed away 12 years ago after an automobile accident, and she had one daughter, who was actively serving in the military overseas, stationed in Iraq. She awoke on a Monday morning not feeling well. She was a bit nauseated with severe heartburn. She had taken an antacid with no relief, and the pain grew worse. Helene had no history of cardiac trouble and was the picture of health for her age, ate right, never smoked, and walked two miles every day, so she did not suspect she was having a heart attack. Eventually, Helene began to feel dizzy and called her physician, Dr. Tondra Washington. Dr. Washington's nurse spoke with Helene and directed her to call 911 immediately.

Helene followed the order to call for help and was transported to Middletown General Hospital. During her initial interview with the nursing staff in the Emergency Department, she indicated that she had a living will and a do not resuscitate order on record at Middletown General from an observation visit three months ago. Helene told the nurse that she had numerous hospitalizations, both inpatient and outpatient, over the past 10 years. Dr. Washington arrived at the emergency room and requested prior records.

Mondays are always very busy in the Health Information Services department at Middletown General Hospital. The call for Helene Maxwell's records was received by Rachelle, who had been with Middletown General for 15 years. It was a routine request for records that appeared, in the computer, to be incomplete and should have been filed in the incomplete record file room. There were deficiencies for two physicians, neither of whom had recently been in to complete their records.

When Rachelle was unable to locate the records in the incomplete file area, she checked the dictating areas, the permanent records room, and areas with charts pulled for studies, and she still had no luck in locating the record. While she was searching, Robert answered a call from the Emergency Department, stating that they needed Mrs. Maxwell's records immediately because they needed the living will and the order for do not resuscitate. Robert began to help Rachelle in the search for the records. They searched the entire department and enlisted the help of other members of the Health Information Services team. Nobody was having any luck, and Dr. Washington came to the department, abruptly stating the urgency of the situation. She had checked with her office staff, and Mrs. Washington had never given them copies of the living will and the do not resuscitate order, so the only known available copy was the one in her hospital records.

Rachelle went to get Marvin, Director of Health Information Services, from an administrative meeting so that he would be aware of the situation and hopefully provide suggestions of additional options to locate the lost record. Meanwhile, Helene Maxwell went into cardiac arrest, and cardiopulmonary resuscitation was initiated because there was not any available documentation to direct otherwise. Helene was intubated and transferred to the intensive care unit with mechanical ventilation.

Dr. Washington had the nursing staff initiate the process to find out how to contact Mrs. Maxwell's daughter, Sarah, in Iraq. She told the nurses that once contact with Sarah was established, she would like to personally talk to her because of the nature of the situation. Eventually, Sarah was located, informed regarding her mother's condition, and plans were in place for her to come home on leave.

When Sarah got home, she searched her mother's house for the original documents and was unsuccessful. She had no idea who her mother's attorney was or whether she had even gone through an attorney to complete the documents. Sarah was upset about the hospital not being able to locate her mother's chart with the do not resuscitate order and living will. By the time she had arrived, Mrs. Maxwell had a feeding tube inserted and was not functioning at all on her own. Sarah was faced with a difficult decision and had no idea what her mother's wishes were in the living will.

Discussion Questions

1. What internal and external forces impact this case?

2. What are the legal issues addressed in this case?

3. What are the ethical issues addressed in this case?

4. How are the ethical issues in this case covered in the American Health Information Management Association Code of Ethics?

5. Using the case method, evaluate possible actions that should be taken and determine the best option.

CASE 8

Which Comes First, the Patient or...

James Sullivan was admitted to Springfield General Hospital on March 15 with chest pain, had a cardiac catheterization that demonstrated significant blockage, underwent a three-vessel coronary artery bypass graft, and experienced numerous postoperative complications that required many returns to surgery. Mr. Sullivan also experienced a cerebrovascular accident that resulted in dysphagia. This led to aspiration pneumonia and respiratory failure, necessitating ventilator support.

Mr. Sullivan was discharged from the acute care unit and admitted to the hospital skilled nursing unit on June 29 for rehabilitation after his hospitalization. The charges on the account for Mr. Sullivan's admission were over $400,000. Coders at Springfield General have always been under a great deal of pressure to keep the inpatient unbilled accounts under $750,000. Prior to Mr. Sullivan's discharge, the unbilled accounts report was at $925,000, and when he was discharged, the amount grew to over a million dollars.

The following morning, the coding supervisor, Carma Davis, was called to meet with Fernando Sanchez, the Chief Financial Officer of Springfield General. He told her that he expected the Sullivan account to be coded and billed before the end of the day because this was a critical financial time for the organization. She assured him that she would personally take care of it.

Carma was well aware of the hospital's financial situation. Weekly analysis of the organization's accounts receivable had recently been replaced with daily analysis and midday reporting of coding productivity. Rumors of layoffs were spreading like wildfire. Carma, being in a lower management position, was in constant fear of her position being eliminated.

Carma felt the need to not only get the account coded, but she also felt she needed to prove her abilities and worth to the organization to Mr. Sanchez. She tracked down the chart immediately after her meeting with Mr. Sanchez and planned to get the chart coded herself. Due to all of the procedures and complicated diagnoses, Carma knew that it would take her most of the day to get the chart coded, especially without being properly assembled and analyzed first.

At 11:30 that morning, James Sullivan was readmitted to acute care with a dissecting abdominal aortic aneurysm, requiring emergency surgery. Dr. Hanson called for the record from the previous hospitalization, which Carma promptly sent to him. Fernando Sanchez contacted Carma at 3:00 p.m. to check the status of the large account on the unbilled accounts list. Carma informed Fernando of the situation, but he was not sympathetic. He insisted that she would stay at work until that account was billed.

Additional complications arose for James Sullivan, and additional specialists were called. Carma made numerous attempts to get the record and was even willing to work on it in an area in the intensive care unit (ICU). Carma went to see Mr. Sanchez regarding the situation, only to be told that it was not his problem how she got the chart done and that he expected that account to be billed before the end of the day.

When Carma went up to the ICU, she encountered a physician who became very angry with her interference with the patient record and told her that financial obligations were not to interfere with patient care needs. Carma returned to her department and was called into her director's office. Keyanna, the Director of Health Information Management at the facility, informed Carma that she had received a call from the ICU nursing supervisor with a complaint about her interfering with patient care to get a chart for coding. Carma told Keyanna that Mr. Sanchez had insisted that the record be coded by the end of the day. Keyanna told Carma that she would contact Mr. Sanchez about the situation and work things out with him.

After Carma went back to her office, Keyanna visited Mr. Sanchez. Keyanna explained that she understood that the Sullivan account was significant on the accounts receivable, but she explained that the patient's health situation required all physicians involved in his care to have immediate access to the health record without interference for administrative financial purposes. However, Mr. Sanchez did not respond sympathetically to the situation, as Keyanna had anticipated. Mr. Sanchez told her that the institution's financial situation was at the point where Full-Time Equivalent (FTE) reduction would be necessary and that if the Sullivan record was not coded and billed by the end of the day, then Keyanna would be required to eliminate Carma's position.

Discussion Questions

1. What internal and external forces impact this case?

2. What are the legal issues addressed in this case?

3. What are the ethical issues addressed in this case?

4. How are the ethical issues in this case covered in the American Health Information Management Association Code of Ethics?

5. Is there anything that Carma could have done differently in this case?

6. How should Keyanna respond to Mr. Sanchez's final statement?

7. What internal and external forces impact this case?

8. What are the legal issues addressed in this case?

9. What are the ethical issues addressed in this case?

10. Using the case method, evaluate possible actions that should be taken and determine the best option.

CASE 9

Physician Access to Information as a Noncustodial Parent

Dr. Singh's 14-year-old son, Rajiv, was recently treated in the Emergency Department. Rajiv's mother has sole custody of Rajiv, and Dr. Singh does not have visitation rights. Due to the circumstances of his divorce, Rajiv's mother provided documentation for inclusion in his health records stating that under no circumstances would Dr. Singh be allowed access to Rajiv's health information. Mrs. Singh's neighbor, Mr. Smith, happened to run into Dr. Singh at the grocery store and asked how Rajiv was recovering. Dr. Singh informed Mr. Smith that he was unaware of any issues concerning Rajiv's health, prompting Mr. Smith to fill him in on the details because Mr. Smith was unaware of the custody arrangements and details of the divorce.

The next morning, Dr. Singh went into the Health Information Services department requesting a copy of his son's records for review. Thanks to Mr. Smith, Dr. Singh was able to provide the date and circumstances of his son's medical treatment to try to lead the staff to believe that he was indeed involved in his son's care. The Release of Information Clerk pulled Rajiv's chart, and as she was getting ready to copy the record, she noticed the note prohibiting Dr. Singh from accessing Rajiv's record. Knowing how easily intimidated this clerk is by confrontation with physicians, he explained that he was simply trying to assist Rajiv's mother by getting a copy of the records to take to a specialist so that she would not have to make the trip to the hospital to attain the records. The file clerk defended the confidential nature of Rajiv's health records and refused to copy the records. Dr. Singh became loud and abrupt with the file clerk to the point that Jane, the Director of Health Information Services, came out of her office to determine what the problem was. Jane reminded Dr. Singh of the confidential nature of all patient health records and the privacy and security issues presented through the Health Information Portability and Accountability Act. Dr. Singh stated that he understood and respected that regulations must be followed.

About 30 minutes later, Dr. Singh presented to the Physician Record Assistant's desk. He requested his incomplete records so that he could sign and dictate outstanding reports. He also requested that the Physician Record Assistant pull Rajiv Jones' chart for him to review. While the Physician Record Assistant was pulling Dr. Singh's records, she encountered difficulty in locating Rajiv's chart. She went to the other areas of the Health Information Services department to see whether anybody else had the chart. When the Release of Information Clerk was approached about the record, she informed the Physician Record Assistant that Dr. Singh was not allowed access to Rajiv's records. The Physician Record Assistant informed Dr. Singh that she could not give him Rajiv's chart, and if he has any questions, he should talk with Jane. Dr. Singh apologized for any inconvenience, completed his incomplete records, and went to the nursing units to do his rounds.

Dr. Singh has developed a relationship of respect with the nurses on the unit and made another attempt at requesting his son's records while on his morning rounds. He asked Betty, a nurse on the orthopedic unit, if she could call to have the chart sent up for him. Betty promptly called Health Information Services, simply stating that a physician needs the chart. The Release of Information Clerk received the call and asked which physician was requesting the records. When she found out that it was Dr. Singh who requested the records, she informed Betty that Dr. Singh was not allowed access to Rajiv's records. Betty responded by demanding that if a physician requests records, that physician's intentions should not be questioned. The Release of Information Clerk finally ended up transferring Betty to Jane, who continued to protect the confidentiality of the records.

After his morning rounds, Dr. Singh stopped in to visit with Charles, the Chief Executive Officer (CEO) of the facility, to make arrangements for their weekly golf outing. During this visit, Dr. Singh made a complaint to Charles regarding the trouble he had encountered trying to get copies of his son's records for his ex-wife so that their son could be seen by a specialist. Immediately after this conversation, Charles appeared in the Health Information Services department to inform Jane that the physicians on staff should be treated with utmost respect and that Dr. Singh was only helping his ex-wife by getting copies of Rajiv's records to be taken to a specialist for follow-up care from his recent ER treatment. When Jane pointed out the note on the record, Charles informed her that because Rajiv's father is a physician that the note did not need to be honored, especially because the request for information was for continuation of care. Jane, confident of her stand on the issue and aware of the consequences of releasing the information, continued to defend the point that the records should not be released to Dr. Singh under any circumstances because of the notice from the patient's mother. Charles requested that Jane leave the chart with him and that his administrative assistant would contact the organization's attorney to clarify whether or not the records should be released with Dr. Singh. Jane was aware of the close relationship between Dr. Singh and Charles and had a gut feeling that if she left the chart with Charles, he would release the information to Dr. Singh. She feared that her job could be in jeopardy if she continued to argue her point with the CEO, yet she wanted to act in an ethical manner and protect the records according to the request for confidentiality by the patient's legal guardian.

Discussion Questions

1. What internal and external forces impact this case?

2. What are the legal issues addressed in this case?

3. What are the ethical issues addressed in this case?

4. How are the ethical issues in this case covered in the American Health Information Management Association Code of Ethics?

5. Did any of the Health Information Management staff members act in an unethical or illegal manner in this case?

6. Indicate how you would have responded if you were the Release of Information Clerk, the physician record assistant, Jane, or the CEO. Justify your answers with legal and ethical rationale.

7. Using the case method, evaluate possible actions that should be taken and determine the best option.

CASE 10

International Release of Information I

Manuel and Sierra Rodrigues were on summer holiday in the United States from Sao Paulo, Brazil. They were doing a great deal of sightseeing, most of their time spent walking. One afternoon during their vacation, the temperature reached 98°F, with a heat index of 110°F. They were trying to pack a lot of activities into the day and had neglected to stop for something to drink. Manuel was feeling the effects of the heat and started to feel light-headed, but he did not say anything to Sierra because he did not want to put a damper on their vacation.

Last year, Manuel had a myocardial infarction. His surgical history includes a three-vessel coronary artery bypass graft and a mitral valve replacement within the past year. Two months ago, he began seeing a different physician after his regular doctor had retired. Manuel's blood pressure had been well-controlled with his medication, but he was having abnormally high readings when he visited the new physician. Because of these high readings, the new physician increased the dosage of his medication and also added a new drug. Manuel had experienced some minor episodes of light-headedness since the change in medications, but with holiday so near, he opted to wait until they returned to Madrid before he would tell his physician about the side effects he had been experiencing.

They continued to walk; eventually, Manuel let Sierra know how he was feeling because he became so dizzy he was unable to see clearly. Sierra suggested they stop to get something to drink and sit for a while, so they found a nearby sidewalk café. Before they could even get to a table, Manuel passed out. The café manager called 911, and he was taken to Northside Hospital.

Sierra and Manuel did not speak much English. Sierra had written out what she thought to be their most pertinent medical information and carried copies in her purse. However, it was written in Portuguese. Northside Hospital's personnel department kept a list of employees who fluently spoke various foreign languages. They had one person who was listed as speaking Portuguese. However, it turned out that she had not used Portuguese recently, and she was a bit rusty. She was able to translate some. The next thing they tried was an online translation tool, which gave them most of what they needed, but still nothing about the new medication.

When Manuel was initially evaluated, his blood pressure was dangerously low. He was determined to be having heatstroke, but he had also developed an abnormal heart rhythm during his time in the emergency department. The emergency department physicians were experiencing great difficulty trying to stabilize Manuel's condition, and his blood pressure abruptly went from excessively low to 220/140. At this point, it was decided that the physicians required more detailed information about Manuel's health history because neither he nor Sierra were able to understand well enough to answer any questions, and a good translator still was not located.

An Internet search brought up a site that indicated there were 713 hospitals in Brazil, with many in the Sao Paulo area. Manuel's health status was becoming more critical, so the emergency department contacted the Health Information Services department to request their assistance in obtaining Manuel's records. The Release of Information Specialist was unsure of how to handle this situation, so she went to *you*, the director, for guidance.

Discussion Questions

1. As Director of Health Information Services at Northside Hospital, how would you handle the situation?

2. Once the hospital with Manuel's records is located, a release of information form must be processed. The emergency department tries to explain your facility's form to Sierra, but she does not understand, and the facility translator's Portuguese is not sufficient to provide her with the information she needs. What are the options at this point?

3. Sierra finally signs your facility's form and you fax it to the hospital in Sao Paulo, Brazil. However, it turns out that your form is not compliant with their needs. They fax you their form to use. What issues may you have to consider with their form?

4. What internal and external forces impact this case?

5. What are the legal issues addressed in this case?

6. What are the ethical issues addressed in this case?

7. How are the ethical issues in this case covered in the American Health Information Management Association Code of Ethics?

8. Using the case method, evaluate possible actions that should be taken and determine the best option.

CASE 11

International Release of Information II

Gretchen Schenck was born in Germany. Her parents moved to the United States when she was 15 years old, leaving a significant amount of close family behind in Wittenberg. Gretchen and her parents traveled to Wittenberg to visit family at least once a year, and she also maintained a close relationship with them via e-mail.

Gretchen became pregnant when she was 25 years old. Soon after that, her grandmother in Germany was diagnosed with cancer that metastasized significantly. Gretchen was admitted to Commontown Hospital early in her pregnancy with a twisted fallopian tube and enlarged ovary that had to be surgically corrected via laparoscopy. Her doctor followed her closely on a weekly basis after her surgery until she completed her first trimester. Her obstetrician was confident that the problem was related to her becoming pregnant but that the problem was fixed to the point where it would not interfere with management of the duration of her pregnancy.

Gretchen was in her fifth month of pregnancy when her grandmother passed away. Her obstetrician cleared her for international air travel so that she could attend her grandmother's funeral. Her flight was uneventful, as was the funeral. She planned to spend two weeks with her family in Wittenberg to help with going through her grandmother's belongings.

While eating dinner at her cousin's house, Gretchen experienced a sharp pain on the same side where she had her laparoscopy for the problems with her ovary and fallopian tube. She laid down, and the pain became increasingly worse later in the evening, so her family took her to the nearest hospital. Luckily, Gretchen's German and English translation skills were excellent, so she was able to explain her condition to the German doctor. She had a sonogram, which revealed that the ovary had become enlarged again. The German doctor wanted to review the records from her previous surgery, so Gretchen filled out a record request form, and the fax number for Commontown Hospital in the United States and for her obstetrician were obtained.

Jasmin was the Release of Information Specialist who received the record request at Commontown Hospital. The first thing she noticed was that the form was not written in English. She took it to Helen, who was director of Health Information Services. Helen contacted the hospital's contracted translator service and was easily able to get an English translation for the record request form.

Helen read the translated document carefully and found that it was not compliant with Health Insurance Portability and Accountability Act (HIPAA) requirements. She contacted the translation service again to have them translate a HIPAA-compliant release of information form into German. The German version of the HIPAA compliant release of information form was faxed to the Wittenberg hospital along with a cover letter that explained why the form they had faxed could not be utilized to release Gretchen's documents.

The Wittenberg hospital responded that they were unable to utilize the U.S. documents because they did not exactly match their organization's guidelines but that they needed Gretchen's records right away because the physician there felt she might need emergency surgery.

Discussion Questions

1. Refer to the document that was sent from the Wittenberg hospital and identify why it is not compliant with HIPAA.

2. If you were in Helen's position, would you have released the records upon receipt of the Wittenberg form? Why or why not?

3. What internal and external forces impact this case?

4. What are the legal issues addressed in this case?

5. What are the ethical issues addressed in this case?

6. How are the ethical issues in this case covered in the American Health Information Management Association Code of Ethics?

7. Using the case method, determine what the best action is at this point.

CASE 12

Compliance Matters

Selena is the Director of Health Information for the Home Health division of Anywhere General Healthcare Systems (AGHS). AGHS is a large health care system that includes a 1,500-bed acute care hospital, home health, a 30-bed skilled nursing unit, a 50-bed rehabilitation unit, and a health insurance provider. There are a number of other smaller hospitals in the same city as AGHS, but none of these hospitals provide comprehensive services as AGHS does.

Selena has been in her position for about one year. Her department consists of four coders, two filing clerks, a receptionist, a Release of Information Specialist, and a scheduler. Selena reports directly to the Home Health Administrator, who reports to the Chief Executive Officer of AGHS. Selena came to AGHS with 15 years of experience in a variety of health information management settings. In addition to her Registered Health Information Administrator credential, she is also a Certified Compliance Professional. Immediately prior to coming to AGHS, Selena worked as a compliance consultant for a nationwide health care consulting firm. Selena is recognized nationwide among her peers and highly respected in the health care community. She has published numerous peer-reviewed articles in professional journals and has coauthored a textbook on compliance. During her interview with AGHS, the administrator informed Selena that the organization could really benefit from her compliance training because they did not yet have a formal compliance program intact. Her predecessor had a general business degree and had no previous experience in the health care environment. He had been unaware of any home health-specific regulations, Health Insurance Portability and Accountability Act (HIPAA), Joint Commission, or Centers for Medicare and Medicaid Services (CMS) guidelines. His job had simply been to manage the office staff and make sure they were doing their jobs. AGHS had decided that it was necessary to hire a credentialed health care professional with knowledge of compliance and other regulatory guidelines because they were aware there were some areas in home health that were noncompliant.

When Selena started at AGHS, she assessed each area of her department to determine opportunities for improvement. The receptionist and scheduling staff all seemed to be doing well in terms of compliance. They had been informed by clinical staff members, plus some had done research on their own regarding home health compliance issues because they knew this was an issue based on what the clinical staff had shared.

When Selena assessed the Release of Information Specialist's work, she was shocked to discover that the individual in this position had no formal training. She had previously been a receptionist and was promoted when the release of information position was vacated. There was no written job description. There were no guidelines previously provided to the Release of Information Specialist addressing the various types of information requests that may be presented. The Release of Information Specialist had never been informed about state laws, national laws, or HIPAA. The Release of Information Specialist informed Selena that her job was simple. When she received a request for records, she copied them and sent them out. If she received a subpoena, she would pass that on to the director, and she had no clue how the records were processed for subpoenas. Selena provided the Release of Information Specialist with appropriate education regarding HIPAA, state laws, and other appropriate issues. A written job description was created, and the Release of Information Specialist demonstrated understanding and agreed to ask Selena if there was ever any question regarding record release.

The filing area was organized, but there was no formal system for chart check-out. Selena initiated a manual sign-out system, which seemed to work well after a couple of weeks. Upon more in-depth assessment of the filing area, Selena discovered that there were unsigned plan of care forms for patients who had most likely been billed. She even found some of these forms that were over a year old and not signed yet. The file room staff members were unaware of the CMS requirements for the plan of care to be signed by the physician prior to billing. Selena initiated a process to ensure timeliness of physician signature for the plan of care forms and communication of signature to the billing office.

The four coders in Selena's department had all been with AGHS for a fairly long time, ranging from 6–25 years in longevity with the organization. She met with each coder individually prior to meeting with the group as a whole. During this assessment, Selena learned that none of the coders had ever gone through any formal coding education. She had concerns about this, along with the fact that there were no credentialed coders on staff. They had all been trained internally. When Selena met with the coders as a group, she informed them that she would be doing an internal audit on their coding. The coders reacted defensively, so Selena explained that the audit was simply a component of the compliance plan that she was working on implementing. This satisfied their concerns, and they were cooperative.

The first month of coding audits demonstrated a 16% accuracy rate for the coders. Selena developed an all-day training session that she required the coders to attend. She reviewed coding conventions and home health billing guidelines. She informed the coders that the audits would continue, and she would watch for trends in the type of errors found and provide monthly education to get the coders compliant. The coders' accuracy improved over time, and eventually, they were at 95% accuracy by the end of the year.

The Home Health Administrator was highly impressed with all of Selena's accomplishments and the changes she had implemented in her first year with the organization. She had thoroughly educated her staff regarding areas of compliance that were previously foreign to them. She developed a comprehensive policy and procedure manual for her department that included specific job descriptions for each position. Selena also compiled a significant start on a compliance manual for the home health division of AGHS from scratch. When setting goals for the following year during her annual evaluation, one of Selena's goals was to generate effective communication between her department and the billing department, which was located in another building. Selena indicated to the administrator that this might help eliminate additional noncompliance issues. Prior to this time, Selena's staff did not realize the relationship between their functions and the functions of the billing department. The administrator agreed that developing communication between the two departments would further reduce compliance issues and encouraged Selena to perform an internal billing audit because the results were so dramatic after initiating the coding audits.

Selena contacted Janet, the Director of Billing, to discuss her plans. Janet was highly cooperative and agreed that the audits would be a positive step toward becoming compliant. Janet was aware of some billing issues that she had tried to point out to the administrator previously and hoped that Selena's audit would help support her concerns. It did not take Selena long at all to discover the issue that Janet had previously addressed.

AGHS Home Health serves a diverse population. This population includes Medicare, Medicaid, self-pay, commercial insurance, elderly, middle-aged, postpartum, and newborn patients. Selena made the observation in her billing audit that none of the visits to the postpartum and normal newborn patients were billed. She discussed this finding with Janet, who informed Selena that she had brought this to the administrator's attention when she started at the organization two years prior. Janet was told that the organization provides complimentary home health visits one week postdischarge for the mothers and babies. Janet told Selena that she did not think much more of the issue because the administrator presented it to her in a manner of confidence that it was acceptable practice. Selena pointed out that because the organization serves Medicare patients, they could not provide a service to anybody else for a lesser charge, and these complimentary visits were definitely less than anything being charged to the Medicare patients.

Selena took her concerns regarding the complimentary visits to the administrator. She was told that the complimentary visits were made for public relations and that they served as a successful marketing tool to bring more business in to the organization. Selena rebutted this statement with providing information to the administrator about the legal implications of providing the complimentary visits for non-Medicare patients. The administrator stated that they would lose too much business if they were to discontinue the complimentary visits and that the issue was nonnegotiable and would not be open for discussion again.

Selena found herself in a situation of noncompliance with nowhere to turn. The organization did not have any form of compliance plan prior to her employment. The administrator had not yet created a position for a compliance officer. There was no means for employees to submit compliance issues. This was the best job Selena had ever had. She would not be able to make nearly as much working in a staff position at any of the other smaller area health care organizations and she was not aware of any openings at the other facilities. She was not comfortable working for an organization that was knowingly acting in a noncompliant manner, and she did not want to risk her future by continuing to be in a position that supported the practice. If the organization were to be sanctioned by the Office of the Inspector General for this situation while she continued to work there aware of the issue, she could lose her compliance credential and could face the possibility of never being able to work for an organization that bills Medicare or Medicaid patients ever again. However, she did not have any other job options at the time.

Discussion Questions

1. What internal and external forces impact Selena's concerns in this case?

2. What ethical concerns are presented in this case?

3. What legal issues need to be considered regarding this case?

4. Outline the information that Selena should include in formal training for newly hired staff in the department related to both legal and ethical issues that should be addressed.

5. How would you handle the situation if you were Selena?

6. What could the administrator do differently in this case?

7. Using the case method, evaluate possible actions that Selena should take and determine the best option.

CASE 13

Will the Real Expert Please Stand Up?

Carmen worked as an education coordinator for a nation-wide health care compliance consulting organization. She had a horribly busy schedule, started work before 8:00 a.m. every day, and rarely finished working until at least 7:00 p.m. every evening. Her husband, Alan, worked at a local factory, and it was difficult for him to get time away as well. Their son was five years old and starting kindergarten the next month.

One of the requirements for kindergarten was documentation of immunization records. Carmen, who provided education on Health Insurance Portability and Accountability Act (HIPAA)-related issues and assisted facilities with form design as part of her job, called Dr. Stallone, her son's pediatrician's, office. Carmen asked Jessica, who answered the phone at Dr. Stallone's office, if she would be able to fax a release of information form to the pediatrician's office and have the office fax the information to her because she was unable to get there during their office hours. Jessica responded by saying, "I'm sorry, honey, but medical records cannot be faxed. It is because of HIPAA." Carmen explained to Jessica that she worked for a health care compliance consulting company, developing education on HIPAA-related issues, and that it was perfectly legal to release information via fax. Jessica corrected Carmen and informed her that she had to go through HIPAA training when she was hired and that there were strict laws about releasing medical information, so she would just have to come in to sign for the records in person.

Carmen decided that she did not have time or energy to argue with Jessica about HIPAA, so she gave up and told her that she would see if she could make other plans. Carmen talked to Alan that evening when she got home from work and asked him if there was any way he could get approval to take a long lunch break to go pick up the records because they needed them for kindergarten registration at the end of the week.

The next evening, Alan informed Carmen that he would be able to take a full hour for lunch the following day to go sign for the records in person. That following morning, Carmen called Dr. Stallone's office, where Jessica answered the phone again. Carmen explained to Jessica that because she could not accept a faxed release of information form, that her husband had made arrangements to take a long lunch to pick up their son's records, and she asked if they could get them prepared ahead of time so that he did not have to wait long when he got there. Jessica responded, "Would it work better for you if I just put the records in the mail for you? We don't even need a signature to mail records."

Discussion Questions

1. Identify the legal and/or ethical issues in this case.

2. What actions might Carmen take in response to her discussions with Jessica?

3. If Carmen gives up and agrees to have Jessica mail her son's immunization records to her, what could the implications be for Jessica and for Dr. Stallone's practice if Carmen were to follow up by filing for a HIPAA violation?

4. Using the case method, evaluate possible actions that should be taken and determine the best option.

CASE 14

A Minor Confidentiality Issue

Six-year-old Tavion Robinson was taken to Methodist Hospital by his father for treatment of a broken arm and abrasions. When asked about the cause of the injury, Tavion's father told the triage nurse that he had fallen from the jungle gym at the park. During the time they were in the emergency department, Tavion's father appeared hesitant to allow Tavion to be left alone with the hospital staff. The emergency department staff suspected that the injuries may not have been acquired in the manner explained by Mr. Robinson. The abrasions were clean, which would not have been the case if Tavion had truly fallen from playground equipment and presented immediately for treatment. When Tavion went for his x-ray, the staff made a point of not allowing his father in the room. They questioned Tavion about his injuries, and he verified his father's explanation. The staff continued to question Tavion, asking if he was ever afraid of being hurt by anybody at home. He consistently denied abuse or fear of abuse, and it was noted as such in his record.

Prior to leaving the Emergency Department, Mr. Robinson requested that a notice be placed in the record that he was to be notified prior to releasing Tavion's records to anybody else. He included in the notice that Tavion's parents are divorced, and his mother, who is the noncustodial parent, may not access Tavion's records without his consent.

The following weekend, Tavion's mother presented to the Health Information department requesting copies of records of the Emergency Department visit. She stated that she suspected his father had been physically abusing him, and she wanted to review the documentation.

Discussion Questions

1. Is Tavion's mother's statement of concern of abuse sufficient to warrant further investigation by the hospital?

2. Should Tavion's mother be directed to a different department of the hospital or another organization regarding her concern of abuse?

3. What internal and external forces impact this case?

4. What are the legal issues addressed in this case? How do your state laws address access to health records by noncustodial parents?

5. What are the ethical issues addressed in this case?

6. How would you respond to Tavion's mother if you were the Release of Information Clerk?

7. Using the case method, evaluate possible actions that should be taken and determine the best option.

CASE 15

Final Lesson Before Graduation

Shandra was a senior in her final semester of the Health Information Management (HIM) program at Anystate University in Smithville. She was completing her final courses, which included Trends in Health Information Management, Organizational Management Theories, and her Professional Practice Experience. Shandra was engaged to Andre, the Assistant Director of Respiratory Therapy at St. James Medical Center, with plans to marry after her graduation. Shandra was carrying a 4.00 grade point average going into her final semester and had hopes of becoming a Health Insurance Portability and Accountability Act (HIPAA) compliance specialist after graduation because she had heard that a new position was being created. She was excited to be able to complete her Professional Practice Experience at St. James Medical Center, the only hospital in Smithville, so she would be able to complete the rest of her courses that same semester, continue to live near her family and fiancé, and hopefully get her foot in the door with a chance at the new HIPAA compliance specialist position.

Shandra started her Professional Practice Experience by attending two full days of orientation with a group of new employees. The orientation sessions included information about infection control, the Occupational Safety and Health Administration, HIPAA, and quality improvement processes. All students and new employees were required to sign confidentiality statements during orientation.

Shandra did exceptionally well completing all of her assigned tasks during her Professional Practice Experience. She also became close with a number of the staff members in the HIM department and in other areas of the facility. She enjoyed being able to take her breaks and lunches with her fiancé and his friends from the hospital.

During breaks and lunches, Shandra overheard a variety of conversations among hospital staff. Occasionally, they would discuss interdepartmental issues, and sometimes they would gossip about hospital staff and physicians. One conversation was focused on a rumor about Henri Pioche, the Director of Respiratory Therapy. Many of the staff members present for the conversation indicated that they heard Mr. Pioche had been diagnosed with some kind of malignant condition and had been recently worked up to determine the possibility of brain metastasis.

Shandra and Andre took their afternoon break alone together that afternoon. Shandra asked Andre if he had heard any kind of confirmation regarding his director's condition. Andre had only heard rumors, but of course, he was curious because he would be the obvious next in line for the director position.

When Shandra returned to the HIM department after break, she pulled up Henri Pioche's records and saw that he had recently had a series of outpatient tests at the facility. She researched further and found that the most recent tests indicated brain metastasis that appeared significant. That evening, Shandra shared her findings with Andre.

The following day, Andre decided to approach Henri about the situation. He simply indicated that he had heard of him having serious health issues. Andre volunteered to help in any way possible and stated he was more than willing to cross-train to expand his duties to be able to cover in case Henri had to be gone for an extended period of time or if anything should happen that he might not be able to return, acting as an interim director until a decision could be made about a replacement.

Henri denied his health issues to Andre. He did not want anybody at St. James to know of his condition, at least not this soon. However, it concerned him that Andre seemed too confident about his knowledge of his health status, so he contacted the Director of Health Information Management to investigate who may have had recent access to his health information.

A report was run to provide an audit log for access to Henri's records, and the HIM department director questioned Shandra to determine why she had been in Henri's electronic health record. Shandra knew immediately that she could not come up with a verifiable excuse, so she decided that honesty was the best policy in this case and admitted that she had looked to see whether what she heard on break was indeed true.

Discussion Questions

1. What impact could Shandra's actions have on her potential employment in any position at St. James Medical Center?

2. What could Shandra do to possibly restore any chance of being hired by St. James Medical Center?

3. Should Shandra be considered for the position of HIPAA compliance specialist after graduation? Why or why not?

4. Should Shandra be allowed to pass her Professional Practice Experience?

5. St. James Medical Center has always had an excellent relationship with Anystate University regarding hosting students and interns. Could this isolated situation be significant enough for the facility to terminate this relationship with the university?

6. What internal and external forces impact this case?

7. What are the legal issues addressed in this case?

8. What are the ethical issues addressed in this case?

9. How are the ethical issues in this case covered in the American Health Information Management Association Code of Ethics?

10. Using the case method, evaluate possible actions that should be taken and determine the best option.

CASE 16

Internal Confidentiality Matters

Brenda Johnson is one of two inpatient coders at Community Hospital. The coders in the Health Information Services department at Community Hospital generally experience poor interpersonal communication within their area of the department. There has been a long-time feeling of distrust and lack of close-knit relationships among the coding staff. Brenda, who is not married, became pregnant and experienced some early complications. She was taken to the Community Hospital ER and was admitted. During her hospitalization, it was determined that her complications were caused by the presence of genital herpes and chlamydia.

Prior to her release from the hospital, Brenda contacted Shirley, the Health Information Services Director at Community Hospital. Shirley met Brenda in her hospital room to discuss arrangements during her absence. Brenda expressed concern specifically regarding having her records sequestered so that her coworkers would not have any access to her information. She stated that she especially did not want any of the coders to have access to her records. Shirley assured Brenda that all staff members in the department were bound to their annual confidentiality statements, that her records would be handled in a professional manner, and that she was overreacting by her response. Brenda stated that she would prefer to process the record herself if it could be sequestered until her return to work.

Shirley agreed to sequester the record until Brenda's return because her physician only ordered her to be off work for one week. However, Brenda developed complications that resulted in additional hospitalization. When Brenda was rehospitalized, she contacted Shirley again, urging her to keep her records secure from the rest of the department. Brenda also indicated to Shirley that this additional hospitalization could potentially last for the duration of her pregnancy. Shirley pointed out to Brenda that it would not be fiscally responsible to hold up billing and additional processing of the record until she returned. Brenda asked Shirley if it would be possible for her to code her previous admission while she was in the hospital and if she could even code her present hospitalization account immediately after her discharge prior to being transported back home. Shirley explained that it would not be appropriate for Brenda to be coding her record while hospitalized; additionally, her current hospitalization record might not be complete enough for coding immediately after her discharge.

Discussion Questions

1. What internal and external forces impact this case?

2. What are the legal issues addressed in this case?

3. What are the ethical issues addressed in this case?

4. How are the ethical issues in this case covered in the American Health Information Management Association Code of Ethics?

5. Is Brenda's request to have her records sequestered appropriate, considering her distrust of her coworkers and the delicate nature of her health status?

6. What implications could there be if Shirley were to allow Brenda to code her own records while in-house and immediately after her discharge?

7. If Brenda were allowed to code her own record while in-house, she would most-likely utilize a code book, rather than an encoder, because she is restricted to her hospital bed. If she were to become injured from lifting the code book and/or chart, what are the liability considerations for the facility?

8. What internal and external forces impact this case?

9. What are the legal issues addressed in this case?

10. What are the ethical issues addressed in this case?

11. Using the case method, evaluate possible actions that should be taken and determine the best option.

CASE 17

The Public Needs to Know...Don't They?

Springfield Memorial is a 300-bed acute care hospital with an addiction recovery center, for which they are well-known throughout the state. Francine was recently hired as clerical support in the Health Information Management (HIM) department. She had attended the two-day new employee house-wide orientation sessions and went through a week of training in the HIM department. One of the other clerical staff members had worked with her for a week to train her for her position, and then she was on her own.

This was Francine's first time working in a health care environment. She felt confident, yet slightly overwhelmed with all of the information she had been exposed to over the past two weeks. She felt especially confused about all of the information she had received regarding Health Insurance Portability and Accountability Act (HIPAA) from both the house-wide orientation and the department orientation. She understood the importance of confidentiality of patient information and the increased safeguards for substance abuse, psychiatric, and human immunodeficiency virus-related information.

It was an election year. Patricia Maxwell was a strong candidate for governor. However, there had been rumors all over the state that she had problems with drinking and gambling. Her husband confronted her about the problem, and she agreed to enter rehabilitation. She chose Springfield Memorial because of their excellent reputation, and it was out of her home town, so recognition chances would hopefully be less.

Patricia took a leave of absence, but she did not provide any details regarding reason or where she could be reached. This unknown leave prompted additional rumors that perhaps she had entered a treatment facility for her rumored drinking and gambling addiction problems. The patient information desks at facilities all over the state were soon swamped with calls requesting information about whether or not Patricia Maxwell was a patient. The Springfield Memorial patient information desk personnel were well-seasoned and would not acknowledge whether or not Patricia Maxwell was a patient at the facility.

One reporter was not satisfied with the response by the information desk, so he called the HIM department. Francine took the call. The reporter asked if she could tell him Patricia Maxwell's room number. Francine was young and not up-to-date on current events, so she did not recognize Patricia Maxwell's name as a candidate for governor and did not suspect anything abnormal about the request for information. Francine looked up the name in the computer and told the person on the phone, who she had assumed was a friend or family member, the room number. She was pleased that this was the first request for a room number that she was able to find on her own without asking for assistance.

The news that evening reported that Springfield Memorial had confirmed that Patricia Maxwell was recently admitted to their addiction recovery unit, which supported the rumors of her alcoholism and gambling habits. The Public Relations Director of the hospital saw the news and was shocked. He had been contacted by several media representatives, but he had denied Patricia Maxwell was a patient at the facility in accordance with HIPAA.

The following day, a department head meeting was called first thing in the morning. All directors at the facility were instructed to question staff members in their department regarding the information leak related to Patricia Maxwell. Aasif Muhamoud, director of HIM, started by talking to his front office staff. Francine responded that she had received a phone call from somebody asking for Patricia Maxwell's room number, but other than that, she had not received any additional calls.

Discussion Questions

1. Francine's error was an honest mistake related to not being familiar with the room numbers for specific units. Discuss what action Asasif should take.

2. How could this information leak have been prevented?

3. What internal and external forces impact this case?

4. What are the legal issues addressed in this case?

5. What are the ethical issues addressed in this case?

6. How are the ethical issues in this case covered in the American Health Information Management Association Code of Ethics?

7. Using the case method, evaluate possible actions that should be taken and determine the best option.

CASE 18

Protecting a Friend

Dr. Adam Marshall is a highly respected surgeon at Uptown General Hospital. He has been on staff for over 20 years with a spotless record. He is well-known in the community for work he does for a variety of charities and medical mission trips he has made. Dr. Marshall goes with a local group of physicians to Zambia twice a year to provide medical care and take much-needed medical supplies. Many of the Zambian patients treated on these mission trips have acquired immune deficiency syndrome (AIDS). Of course, all of the physicians take necessary precautions when treating these patients.

During a recent mission trip, Dr. Marshall took a break to do some sightseeing. While he was out, he collapsed due to heat and dehydration and suffered a significant laceration on his arm. A local woman aided Dr. Marshall, treated his wound temporarily, and took him to the hospital for further treatment. What Dr. Marshall did not know was that the woman who assisted him had full-blown AIDS. He was so concerned about his injury that he paid no attention to the woman's hands and forearms, which had ulcerated areas that were oozing.

The following week, the woman who treated Dr. Marshall was brought into the mission clinic for AIDS treatment. Dr. Marshall did not think much of it because there was minimal contact when the woman helped him. However, three weeks later, Dr. Marshall developed some mild flu-like symptoms and thought the worst case scenario. He confided in Dr. Singh, one of his colleagues working at the mission clinic, and explained how the woman had treated his open wound and that he was concerned about exposure. Dr. Singh did human immunodeficiency virus (HIV) testing, which confirmed that Dr. Marshall had indeed contracted the disease from the woman who had helped him.

Dr. Marshall and Dr. Singh were close friends from their days in medical school. Because testing was done outside of the United States, the physicians did not make an official report. They had a gentleman's agreement that the incident would not be discussed in their hometown, especially at the hospital, to maintain Dr. Marshall's respected status.

About a year later, Dr. Marshall had reported to work in the surgery department at Uptown General on a day that he had waken up not feeling well. It was not a major illness, but Dr. Marshall was experiencing some lightheadedness, so he decided it was not necessary to reschedule his cases for the day. All went well most of the morning until Dr. Marshall experienced his first ever surgical mishap. He experienced a brief period of blacking out, during which his hand slipped with the scalpel, cutting through his gloves and making a large laceration that immediately bled profusely into the patient's surgical site. The scalpel did not cause any accidental lacerations for the patient. Dr. Singh had been called in to assist by finishing the procedure and closing the patient because Dr. Marshall was taken to rest, and the remainder of his cases were rescheduled because of his feelings of illness that day.

Discussion Questions

1. Should Dr. Marshall inform the hospital and/or the patient regarding his HIV status after this incident? Justify your answer.

2. If Dr. Marshall does not inform anybody about his HIV status, should Dr. Singh? Why or why not?

3. Should the patient be informed regarding Dr. Marshall's accident in surgery because there was no apparent injury to the patient at the time? Why or why not?

4. What internal and external forces impact this case?

5. What are the legal issues addressed in this case?

6. What are the ethical issues addressed in this case?

7. How are the ethical issues in this case covered in the American Health Information Management Association Code of Ethics?

8. Using the case method, evaluate possible actions that should be taken and determine the best option.

CASE 19

What Next?

Belinda had worked at Sunset Hills Hospital for 12 years, and she was an excellent coder in the Health Information Management (HIM) department. She was happily married to her husband of 16 years and had a daughter who had recently gotten her learner's permit for driver's education. Aside from her immediate family, Belinda did not have any other relatives. Her father passed away when she was in high school, and her mother had recently died unexpectedly from a massive stroke the previous month. Since the death of her mother, Belinda had somewhat isolated herself from most of her close friends, mainly because she was busy taking care of cleaning out her mother's house and tying up loose ends with the rest of the estate.

Saturday afternoon, her daughter needed hairspray before getting ready to go to prom. Belinda's husband needed some items from the store as well, so he went with her and allowed her to drive. This was her daughter's first time behind the wheel. She was both excited and nervous. They lived in a rural area and had quite a distance to drive to get to the closest store. Her father was proud of how well she was doing thus far. They reached a section of the road with deep ravines on either side. Two vehicles were approaching from the opposite direction. The one vehicle in back got over into the daughter's lane to try to pass the other vehicle and was speeding directly toward her in her lane. There was nowhere for Belinda's daughter to go, and she and Belinda's husband were hit head-on by the vehicle, which was estimated to be moving at a speed around 90 miles per hour. Belinda's husband and daughter were pronounced dead at the scene of the accident.

Belinda took a week off for the funeral preparations and to take care of things at home with insurance and going through her husband and daughter's things. Steven, the director of HIM, told Belinda that she could take off as much time as she needed. Her coworkers, who had become some of her best friends over the years, all helped her as much as possible. She insisted on only taking one week off because she wanted to be busy and keep her mind off of things. Steven talked to Belinda about the organization's employee assistance program, which provided free counseling services to employees in need, but she refused, continuing to insist that she was fine.

Belinda was far from fine, but she was not the type of person who was comfortable depending on anybody else for help. She presented herself well at work, almost too well, but as soon as she got home, her evenings were spent in tears. This continued for weeks until June 12, which would have been her daughter's 16th birthday. She had not slept well at all the night before, knowing that it would be a difficult day for her to face. She finally got out of bed at 5:00 a.m., tired of tossing and turning. She went into her daughter's bedroom, which was still mostly intact as her daughter had left it. She was drawn to one of her daughter's favorite pictures, sitting on her vanity. It was a photograph of her husband and daughter at her daughter's 15th birthday at Belinda's mother's house. She sat and wept, holding the picture for over an hour. She missed her family, and the depression had become more than she could handle.

Belinda thought that maybe she would feel a little better after a shower. She went into the bathroom, which had a double vanity. She looked over to the side that used to be where her husband would be getting ready for work with her in the morning. All of his things were still there. She walked over and started picking up a few of his personal items, when she found his blood pressure medication. It was at this point when Belinda decided that she could not take another day of being alone, without her daughter, husband, and mother. It was unclear how many pills Belinda had taken. She went into the kitchen and drank an undetermined amount of wine as she wrote a note for anyone who would find it. She had stopped going to church and did not socialize with anybody at this point. Outside of work, she had shut out all of her friends.

Belinda was surprised at how well she felt for what seemed to be an eternity because she had taken her husband's medication and had been drinking on top of that. Eventually, she became incredibly dizzy, lightheaded, and she started to have second thoughts. Belinda called 911, but she did not stay on the line as she was instructed while help was on its way. She went into the living room onto the sofa, feeling more and more lightheaded. The emergency response team had to force their entry because Belinda was unconscious when they arrived. She was taken to Sunset Hills and admitted to the intensive care unit (ICU) in critical condition.

Belinda had never been a patient at Sunset Hills before, and she did not know many staff members outside of her department. The police had located her purse, which contained identification, but she did not have her insurance card in there for some reason. The only numbers she had in her cell phone were those of her husband, daughter, and mother. They checked with neighboring residents, but living in a rural area, they had never taken the chance to meet any of their neighbors, most of whom were new to the area. Much effort was placed on attempting to locate next of kin while Belinda was comatose in the ICU on a ventilator with a feeding tube.

Sara did census and statistics in the Health Information Management department. She was well-respected by her peers for her high sense of work ethic. Sara noticed Belinda's name on the census sheet for ICU with an admission diagnosis of suicide attempt, but she did not mention it to anybody, including Steven. She assumed that Steven had already been notified of the situation.

A week passed, and Belinda had not only missed work, but she did not call in. Although Steven was concerned, he was also angry that Belinda was not returning any of the phone messages he had left for her. One of the other inpatient coders was on vacation, and another had to take time off for an unexpected family funeral that week. Steven had administration on his back about the quickly increasing inpatient accounts receivable, and he was forced to complete termination paperwork to submit to Human Resources for Belinda so he could replace her position. Although coders are generally difficult to replace, the timing seemed to be perfect for Steven. When he took the paperwork into the Human Resources department, he was informed that there was a woman in the other room completing an application for a coding position, should one ever become available. Steven interviewed her as soon as she completed her application. Her husband was transferred to Sunset Hills, and she was an experienced coder with Registered Health Information Technician and Certified Coding Specialist (CCS) credentials. She took a coding test and did amazingly well, so he hired her.

The following week, Belinda's condition improved, and she awoke. Her endotracheal tube and feeding tube were removed, and when she learned where she was, she asked one of the nurses to contact Steven and request that he come up to see her. Steven was shocked to learn what had happened with Belinda. She shared with him that she would soon be transferred to a regular room, where she would be for another day or two, and then she would be released to home. She told him that a psychiatrist was treating her and that she would be continuing to see him on an outpatient basis after her discharge. Belinda told Steven that her doctor, who was unaware until that day that Belinda was a hospital employee, was not going to make her take additional time off work after her discharge and that she was looking forward to returning to work because that was the only stable area of her life.

Discussion Questions

1. How should Steven respond?

2. Should Sara have informed Steven when she saw Belinda's name on the ICU census? Why or why not?

3. What are the legal and ethical issues for all involved?

4. Using the case method, determine what the best action is at this point.

CASE 20

On the Floor

Lise has worked in the health information management field for almost 20 years, all of which has been spent working at Community Medical Center in various positions. She started as a file clerk when she was in college and worked her way up to Director of Health Information Services. She has a master's degree in Health Services Administration and is currently working on a PhD in Health Care Policy. She shares her expertise with new employees by providing orientation and continuing education sessions about Health Insurance Portability and Accountability Act, privacy, and security. Over the years, Lise has become well-respected among her peers and staff at all levels at Community Medical Center.

Lise's father has a history of lung cancer, for which he had previously had a lobectomy and chemotherapy. Lise was spending the evening with her parents, when her father began to exhibit symptoms consistent of a stroke. Her parents only lived two blocks from Community Medical Center, so she drove them to the Emergency Department, through which her father was admitted. The physician in the Emergency Department ordered a computed tomography (CT) scan of his head, which showed an abnormal area that was not well-defined. Her father's primary care physician reviewed the CT and explained to Lise and her mother that there was an area of abnormality; however, they were unable to determine whether it was a mass or hemorrhage. Because of the undetermined behavior of the abnormal area, a neurologist and oncologist were both called for consultation.

The following day was exhausting and confusing for Lise and her parents. Her father's primary care physician re-reviewed the CT, as did the neurologist and oncologist. They went back and forth among each other regarding the nature of the anomaly on the CT, so it was eventually decided to order magnetic resonance imaging (MRI). The MRI added more stress to the situation because Lise's father was dreadfully claustrophobic, yet he refused sedation because he wanted to be completely alert to receive his test results. The MRI was attempted without medication, but sedation was necessary. After the test, the neurologist and oncologist both visited Lise's father and discussed their interpretations with the family. Unfortunately, they still differed in their opinions.

Lise's mother stepped out of the room to go to the public restroom. A few minutes later, Lise stepped out to go make a phone call. When she walked down the hall, she discovered her mother at the nursing station looking at a chart that was on the counter. The unit secretary had gone to lunch, and no nursing staff members were around. Lise approached her mother about looking at the chart. Her mother explained that she saw Lise's father's chart sitting out, and she wanted to see for herself what the reports said and what the doctors were really saying. Lise continued to attempt to get the chart away from her mother. While Lise and her mother were disputing the issue of accessing her father's chart, Ricardo Diaz, the Director of Nursing, came to the nursing unit desk.

When Ricardo appeared, Lise had managed to intercept her father's chart from her mother, and she was still holding it. After Lise and Ricardo had exchanged greetings, Ricardo asked Lise how her father was doing; then, Ricardo noticed that Lise was holding her father's chart. He asked her to put the chart down, then took her to the private family conference area on the floor to discuss that it was not appropriate for her to review her father's chart. He expressed his disappointment that she, of all people, should know better. Lise tried to explain that she was simply getting the chart away from her mother, but Ricardo would not accept the explanation.

Discussion Questions

1. What would your next action or response be if you were in Ricardo's position? Justify your response.

2. What would your next action or response be if you were in Lise's position? Justify your response.

3. How might future similar incidents be prevented?

4. What internal and external forces impact this case?

5. What are the legal issues addressed in this case?

6. What are the ethical issues addressed in this case?

7. How are the ethical issues in this case covered in the American Health Information Management Association Code of Ethics?

8. Using the case method, determine what the best action is at this point.

CASE 21

Protection of Passwords

Janet worked as the second shift supervisor in the Memorial Hospital Health Information Services department. She had been in her position for 10 years. Her position was responsible for supervision of three transcriptionists, two assembly and analysis specialists, and two record retrieval clerks. She also did quality assurance on completed records prior to filing in the permanent file room. During her shift on a fairly quiet Wednesday evening, Dr. Ahmed Kumar came in with a request she was unsure how to handle. Dr. Kumar, the chairman of the mortality review committee, was escorted into Janet's office by Kate, one of the record retrieval clerks. Kate appeared upset, and Dr. Kumar was acting impatient because Kate was unable to accommodate his needs.

Dr. Kumar informed Janet that one of Dr. Ali Shah's patients has just expired in a manner similar to two other recent deaths in his patients. The clinical staff on the patient care unit notified Dr. Kumar because they recognized similar circumstances with the previous deaths and alerted him to the possibility that similar deaths might have occurred a number of other times over the past two years. Dr. Kumar demanded that records for all of Dr. Shah's patients who have expired needed to be pulled for him to review immediately. Janet explains to Dr. Kumar that she does not have access to run the report in the computer to get the list of Dr. Shah's patients. Dr. Kumar does not back down on his request to have the records pulled immediately and tells Janet to find somebody who can get them. Janet calls Christine, the Health Information Management Director, regarding the situation. Christine lives over an hour away from Memorial Hospital and is a single parent with her children in bed. She did not have immediate access to a babysitter due to the late hour and did not want to get her kids out of bed to go to the hospital to run the report herself. Christine tells Janet that she will give her the access code and instructions to run the report.

Janet indicates to Christine that she is not comfortable about having Christine's computer access code for a number of reasons. She asks Christine whether there is anybody else who has access and might be able to come in to run the report. Christine insisted that Janet follow her directions and run the report herself using Christine's access code.

Janet used Christine's access to pull the records requested by Dr. Kumar. After Dr. Kumar left the department, Janet curiously went through the menu on the computer to see what functions Christine had access to and the function of each one. Janet, however, did not want to betray Christine's trust and did not get into any information that she felt would be inappropriate.

The following afternoon, Dave, the Director of Information Services, contacted Christine. Dave informed Christine that a routine review of staff access indicated that she had been in the system the previous night, and he provided a list of functions that had been accessed.

Discussion Questions

1. What internal and external forces impact the concerns of each person in this case?

2. What ethical concerns are presented in this case?

3. What legal issues need to be considered regarding this case?

4. Which of the characters in this case acted in an unethical manner?

5. What could have been done differently?

6. Did Janet act appropriately by agreeing to run the report according to Christine's orders?

7. How are the issues in this case addressed by the American Health Information Management Association Code of Ethics?

8. Using the case method, evaluate possible actions that should be taken by Christine and determine the best option.

CASE 22

Electronic Health Record Security

Marissa Harris worked in the Information Services department for Smallville Hospital. The hospital is a small 75-bed acute care facility in a town of 6,400. She had 20 years experience and a bachelor's degree in Health Information Management (HIM) with a currently maintained Registered Health Information Administrator credential. Her experience in HIM was diverse, including coding, management, and performance improvement positions in a variety of health care settings. She recently completed a master's degree in Health Care Informatics and was transferred to the position of Electronic Health Record (EHR) Coordinator at Smallville Hospital in the past year. Her position included 24-hour on-call assistance for any issues related to EHRs at the facility.

Marissa's mother, Mildred, had multiple health issues, and she had recently moved in with Marissa and her husband because she was no longer able to live on her own. Marissa's mother had the reputation of being the Smallville town gossip and took pride in being the first to know any news to share with her young-at-heart group at church.

Marissa received a call one evening regarding an issue with the EHR system, which required her to connect to the system from home. She utilized a virtual private network (VPN) to connect to the facility, with additional layers of password-protected security to access the records. Marissa had finally corrected the EHR problem and was getting ready to check one more thing before logging out when she heard her mother scream for help in the other room. Marissa quickly ran to her mother's aid, finding that her husband had collapsed, fallen down the stairs, and was unconscious. Marissa called 911, and the paramedics thought that her husband had suffered a myocardial infarction. Marissa followed the ambulance to the hospital, leaving her mother at home. She had completely forgotten that she was still signed into the VPN and EHR system.

While Marissa was at the hospital with her husband, her mother wandered into Marissa's office and noticed that the computer was still logged into the hospital system. Mildred was curious about this new EHR system her daughter was working on and innocently checked out what it could do. While she was surfing the EHR system, she recalled that the pastor of her church had recently been on leave for three weeks and had not shared the details of his absence. Some of the ladies in her young-at-heart group were worried that he may have been out for health reasons, so Mildred searched the EHR database for his name. Sure enough, there was a record for her pastor during the time he was on leave. Mildred opened the record to read it, and as she read through the details of her pastor's record, she learned that he had lung cancer with brain metastasis.

Mildred could not believe her pastor had not told the congregation about his very serious health condition. She was deeply concerned for the well-being of her pastor and felt that it was her duty to immediately put him on the church prayer chain. The following day, Mildred's pastor received a call from a member of the prayer chain, expressing concern about his cancer and asking if there was anything she could do to help. Pastor Martin had no idea how any of his parishioners found out about his condition because he had not shared details with anybody. He called the hospital to find out whether they could track who had accessed his records. A report was run and tracked that Marissa's log-on was the most recent to access the record.

Marissa was still at the hospital and had spent the night in intensive care unit (ICU) at her husband's bedside. Not only had her husband suffered a massive myocardial infarction, but he also had a traumatic cerebral hemorrhage from falling down the stairs. The doctors had just informed her that the damage was irreversible, and he would be unable to survive without dependence on life support. They had discussed the alternatives, and a decision was made to take him off of the ventilator.

Sari, the Chief Information Officer at Smallville Hospital, was notified of the EHR access issue for Pastor Martin's records. Sari was aware that Marissa was in the ICU with her husband, but she did not know the severity of his condition. Sari went to the ICU to talk with Marissa regarding the access issue, only to find Marissa weeping at her husband's side because the physician just pronounced death shortly after removing him from mechanical assistance.

Discussion Questions

1. How should Sari approach the situation?

2. What could have been done to prevent the security breach?

3. What internal and external forces impact this case?

4. What are the legal issues addressed in this case?

5. What are the ethical issues addressed in this case?

6. How are the ethical issues in this case covered in the American Health Information Management Association Code of Ethics?

7. Using the case method, evaluate possible actions that should be taken and determine the best option.

CASE 23

A "Free" Gift

Jasmin had worked in the health information management field for 20 years. She had spent the past five years working for a compliance consulting organization. Her client base consisted of hospitals, physician offices, and long-term care facilities in her state. Her husband, Raphael, worked in the maintenance department for a local health care facility, which included a hospital and attached building with independent physician offices. Jasmin and Raphael had three children. Their oldest two children had their own personal computers, and their youngest, who was in third grade, had been asking for her own. Their financial situation did not allow them the ability to purchase another computer at the time.

One day at work, Raphael was sent to pick up some large items to take to the dumpster from one of the physician's offices. When Raphael got to the physician's office, he was directed to a counter where there were three computers that were going to the dumpster. Out of curiosity, Raphael asked the office manager what was wrong with them. Sylvia, the office manager, stated that the computers were fine, and they had simply upgraded to newer computers in their office. Raphael asked if they had considered selling the old computers, and Sylvia responded that if he knew of somebody who could use them, to take them and just give away the computers.

Raphael took two of the computers to the dumpster and one of them to his car to take home. The timing could not have been better because his youngest daughter's birthday was in two days, and this computer would be the perfect gift for her.

When Raphael got home from work, his daughter was thrilled about the new computer. He explained to her that they would have to make sure everything worked before they could set it up in her room. That night, Raphael and Jasmin set up the computer in the kitchen and started to check out what they might need to get it in working condition for their daughter. The computer worked very well. Jasmin noticed an icon on the desktop for scheduling software. She opened the program, concerned that the office had left patient information loaded. Fortunately, she was unable to open any patient information in the program.

Raphael had been taking night classes at a local community college, working on a Management Information Systems degree. He checked things out further on the computer, finding that all of the patient files were in the recycle bin on the computer. Jasmin told Raphael that she was glad he thought to check there and that they were able to delete the files. Raphael explained to Jasmin that emptying the recycle bin would not completely eliminate the data. He told her that the entire hard drive would need to be erased and reformatted. Jasmin responded that she would feel better about having the information properly removed from the computer. However, Raphael pointed out that after erasure and reformatting, they would have to install an operating system, such as a licensed copy of Windows, which would cost $200 to $300.

Discussion Questions

1. Did Raphael do anything wrong by taking the computer home? Why or why not?

2. How would you have responded if you were in Jasmin's position?

3. What internal and external forces impact this case?

4. What are the legal issues addressed in this case?

5. What are the ethical issues addressed in this case?

6. How are the ethical issues in this case covered in the American Health Information Management Association Code of Ethics?

7. Using the case method, determine what the best action is at this point.

CASE 24

Two Halves Do Not Always Make a Whole

Esther Simpson was a patient in the ambulatory surgery department at St. Joseph's Hospital. She was to have a tonsillectomy and adenoidectomy performed by Dr. Bradley. Her pretesting results were normal, and she was prepped and proceeded to surgery. The left tonsil and adenoid were removed. Then, Esther started hemorrhaging profusely as Dr. Bradley started the excision on the right side. Dr. Bradley ended up calling in Dr. Wilson to assist due to the complicated nature of her bleeding. Once hemostasis was achieved, Dr. Bradley decided to terminate the procedure and remove the remaining tonsil and adenoid at a later date.

Lesley Parker, Registered Health Information Administrator, CCS, received Esther Simpson's record for coding a couple of days after her surgery. She assigned the appropriate code for the procedure, along with the appropriate modifier to accurately reflect that the initially intended procedure was not carried out to completion.

Follow-up lab work two weeks later indicated that Esther would be a stable surgical candidate to return for the removal of the remaining tonsil and adenoid. Dr. Bradley performed the procedure without complication. Lesley received this chart for coding and assigned the appropriate procedure codes and modifier for the procedure performed.

Two weeks later, Lesley received a call from Alice at Dr. Bradley's office. Alice informed Lesley that she had been in contact with Esther's insurance company and that the hospital coded Esther's accounts inappropriately. She stated that for Dr. Bradley to receive proper payment for his services, the hospital codes must not contradict the codes assigned by his office. Lesley pulled the records and indicated to Alice the rationale for her code assignment. Alice explained to Lesley that she should not assign any modifiers, code both encounters as if the procedure was completed, and that she was going to write a letter to the insurance company stating that the hospital coded both cases incorrectly.

Discussion Questions

1. What is the correct code assignment in this case?

2. How should Lesley proceed to follow up if Alice writes to the insurance company regarding the inconsistency in code assignment?

3. What internal and external forces impact this case?

4. What are the legal issues addressed in this case?

5. What are the ethical issues addressed in this case?

6. Using the case method, evaluate possible actions that should be taken and determine the best option.

CASE 25

If It Was Documented, Was It Done?

Dr. James Gottrocks is a plastic surgeon who does all of his procedures at Beachside General Hospital. He has an excellent reputation as a surgeon and has been in practice for 25 years. He serves a large population of Medicare patients for a variety of skin disorders resulting from years of sun exposure.

Dr. Gottrocks is well-known in the health care community for his meticulous work as a surgeon. Health care workers in the community also know him for his arrogant and sometimes harsh attitude. He will only work with specific operating room personnel, and his scrub nurse has been with him for the entire 25 years he has been in practice. The staff members in the operating room are accustomed to his military style of ordering assistance and supplies and have established a deep sense of respect for him as a surgeon. The staff members in the Health Information Services department are often intimidated by his mannerisms, and some perceive him as mean. Dr. Gottrocks not only prides himself in his work as an accomplished plastic surgeon, but also in his extensive knowledge in all areas of practice management. He proclaims himself to be a self-taught coder and assigns codes on all of his office records, claiming that this method of coding is the only way that a physician can receive truly accurate reimbursement.

The coding policy at Beachside General states that any time a physician appends a record, that record shall be returned to the coding staff to determine whether any coding changes are necessary. The coders had recently discussed a trend they had noticed with the charts being returned to them. It seemed to them as if most, if not all, the records of Dr. Gottrocks come back to the coders after he completes his deficiencies. Further discussion found that they all seemed to be finding documentation appended that supports a higher level code on all of his records they have been getting back. One of the coders took this concern to Melissa, the Director of Health Information Services. Melissa, realizing that the coders are among the staff in her department who do not seem to like Dr. Gottrocks, responded to the coders' concerns as trying to find something wrong with him and assured them that he is simply a physician who actually understands the ins and outs of coding and documentation and that they should appreciate his attention to detail.

The coders were not satisfied with this response. Brenda, one of the coders, has a close friend, Suzanne, who works as a surgical technician in the ambulatory surgery department. Brenda shares her concerns with Suzanne, who agrees that the documentation practices of Dr. Gottrocks do not sound completely honest. Dr. Gottrocks dictates his operative reports in a record completion area in the ambulatory surgery department. Suzanne, in response to her discussion with Brenda, listens to Dr. Gottrocks dictate his reports the following day. She feels that his dictation is completely accurate. Brenda notes the patients on the surgery schedule that day, and the coders watch for the records to come back with appended notes.

The following week, Dr. Gottrocks comes in to complete his deficient records. The records are all returned to the coding staff with appended operative notes. Brenda calls Suzanne about the changes that were noted. Suzanne confirms that the appended reports indicate that a greater procedure was performed than what was actually done by Dr. Gottrocks. Brenda thanks her for her help and states that she is going to make sure this practice is stopped. Suzanne fears that her involvement in the situation could have a negative impact on her position and asks Brenda not to let her supervisor know where she got her information.

Discussion Questions

1. Could the current practice of changing documentation of Dr. Gottrocks continue to occur once the facility migrates to utilizing a completely EHR?

2. What steps could be taken to monitor the changes while still utilizing hard-copy paper documents?

3. What internal and external forces impact the concerns of each person in this case?

4. What ethical concerns are presented in this case?

5. What legal issues need to be considered regarding this case?

6. Using the case method, evaluate possible actions that should be taken by Brenda and determine the best option.

CASE 26

Who's the Coder?

St. Ann's Hospital is a 150-bed acute care facility in the Midwest. The facility case mix index averages around 1.850. There are four inpatient coders and five outpatient coders on staff at St. Ann's, and most have been with the organization for more than five years. All of the coders at St. Ann's hold American Health Information Management Association (AHIMA) credentials, many of them having both Registered Health Information Administrator and CCS or Registered Health Information Technician and CCS.

St. Ann's has both inpatient and outpatient regular coding audits done on a quarterly basis. These audits are performed by an external organization that is a nationwide consulting firm. The audits address coding accuracy, appropriateness of documentation, optimal and appropriateness of reimbursement, and opportunities for education of coding staff and physicians. The results of the coding audits at St. Ann's consistently demonstrate that the coders are performing at a 99% accuracy rate.

The coding staff at St. Ann's has worked closely with the national consulting firm to ensure that their physician query process is appropriate, compliant, and thorough. The coders at St. Ann's have developed an excellent rapport with the medical staff, and the physician query process operates in an efficient manner, with less than a 24-hour turnaround time. The coders are well-informed regarding how to present a physician query in a non-leading manner, maintaining the physician's role as the decision-maker.

Administration at St. Ann's was contacted by Omar Shariff. Omar is a registered nurse who proposed to the administrators of St. Ann's that he could implement a program that would improve reimbursement for the organization through improved provider documentation. Omar informed them that he had implemented the program at similar facilities and provided statistical information reflecting the change in reimbursement. Omar explained that he had thoroughly researched St. Ann's practices and provided an estimate of the amount of increased reimbursement that they could anticipate utilizing his program. The administrators were impressed with his proposal, and they were in the process of reorganizing the case management department, so they created a new position for Omar Shariff.

Omar's program was based on transferring all inpatient coding responsibilities from the coders in the Health Information Services department to the case management nursing staff on the patient care units. The rationale was that physician query could be performed concurrently during the hospitalization of the patients, so that late documentation after discharge would not indicate inadequate documentation reflective of poor care. Omar undertook the task of training the case management nursing staff how to code in two, four-hour sessions. He assured administration that his staff would fully understand all they needed to know about coding and Diagnosis Related Group assignment for optimal reimbursement.

Roxanne, the Director of Health Information Services, was informed by administration about the new concurrent program that would be implemented. She was told that this change was not negotiable and that her staff must adjust accordingly to their change in duties. Roxanne met with her inpatient coding staff to communicate the changes as they were outlined by administration. They would no longer be doing any actual coding;

rather, their job descriptions changed to case abstracting and data entry. Roxanne shared the multiple concerns expressed by her coding staff. The concerns expressed by the coders included:

- Omar does not hold any formal coding credentials.
- The case management nurses have never had any other coding education.
- Coding is not something that can be learned and mastered in two, four-hour sessions.
- The existing coding staff members at St. Ann's have AHIMA credentials that indicate they are at mastery level in their coding skills.
- Coding audits from a nationwide consulting firm indicate that the existing coding staff members have consistently been coding at 99% accuracy.
- Case management nurses have not had formal education regarding coding and reimbursement compliance, creating potential for noncompliant coding practice.
- What would happen to the existing coders' jobs?

Roxanne recognized that she had expressed the same concerns to administration when she was informed about the change and that this was not negotiable. She assured them that they would not be laid off as the result of the changes. The volume of outpatient encounters had increased so that some of the coders would be transferred to the outpatient coding area, and the rest would work on data entry.

Two of the inpatient coders resigned immediately, accepting positions at other local hospitals. The remaining coders continued to pursue compliance concerns with the changes being made and to research Omar's history. They learned through their local network that Omar had implemented his program in four other hospitals in the state and been terminated shortly after each time. Eventually, they learned that he had been associated with a consulting firm that had been cited for fraudulent coding practices. The coders took these concerns to Theresa and then to the compliance officer and administration. They were repeatedly told that Omar had gone through a background check prior to his employment and that nothing significant turned up.

The previous coders who had since become abstractors for the cases coded by the case management nurses noted many significant errors in coding. The errors included the following:

- Sequencing principal diagnosis other than what was indicated by the attending physician without approval
- Case management nurses writing diagnoses on the face sheet and coding without physician approval
- Physician query forms written with blatantly leading questions
- Incorrect code assignment
- Missing codes for complications and comorbid conditions

The abstractors took a sampling of the records with the errors to Theresa, the compliance officer, and the organization administrators. They were told that their jobs were no longer to code and that they should not be wasting time evaluating the work of the case managers. In response, the abstractors developed low morale and a decreased sense of loyalty to St. Ann's.

Discussion Questions

1. What additional "flags" should Theresa be suspicious of in this case?

2. Are there any issues presented in this case that are not in compliance with the AHIMA Code of Ethics?

3. Does Theresa have a legitimate case regarding the changes?

4. What internal and external forces impact the concerns of the inpatient coders in this case? Theresa's concerns?

5. What ethical concerns are presented in this case?

6. What legal issues need to be considered regarding this case?

7. Using the case method, evaluate possible actions that St. Ann's should take and determine the best option.

CASE 27

New Kid on the Block

Shondra Johnson is a new graduate of a Health Information Technology program. She successfully passed her Registered Health Information Technician (RHIT) exam three months ago. She was hired by Springfield General Hospital as an outpatient coder immediately after passing her RHIT exam. This is Shondra's first "real job," and she has a high sense of determination to be successful. Shondra thoroughly read all of the policy and procedural manuals during her orientation, taking notes and paying close attention to details outlined in the organizational compliance manual.

During her training period, Shondra worked with Geoffrois, an experienced outpatient coder who has been at Springfield General for 18 years. Geoffrois reinforced the coding policy that Shondra reviewed, especially regarding productivity and the unbilled accounts report. It was obvious to Shondra that this organization wanted to keep their unbilled accounts to a minimum. Springfield General's unbilled accounts at this time were at an all-time high, especially the outpatient accounts, because they had been short-staffed in the outpatient coding area for six months.

Shondra encountered several outpatient records with questionable documentation during her training period. Rather than showing Shondra how to handle these records, Geoffrois simply took them and told Shondra that he would handle them and show her at a later date what to do with them after they were working with less of a coding backlog. Shondra did not question Geoffrois about this because she just thought that he was helping to reduce the outpatient coding backlog.

Another occurrence during Shondra's training period that she did not question was calls from the outpatient billing department that Geoffrois insisted on handling. Geoffrois would not allow Shondra to answer the phone, telling her that it would be more efficient if he would handle the calls on his own because some of them were complicated and required the knowledge of an experienced coder. This explanation made sense to Shondra, who wanted to focus on mastering her current tasks.

Two months had passed, and Geoffrois had to leave town for a death in his family. Shondra was comfortable with her outpatient coding duties and thought all would go well during Geoffrois' absence. In fact, she secretly enjoyed having some time to do her job without Geoffrois hovering over her every second. All was going smoothly until the phone rang in the outpatient coding area. Shondra was excited to finally have the opportunity to take care of one of the phone requests that Geoffrois had reserved only for himself. The call was from Annette, one of the Medicare billing representatives. Annette requested that Shondra remove a V code from an account because Medicare would not pay the account with the code on it. Shondra took down the information and told Annette that she would get back to her. Shondra pulled the record and determined that the V code was necessary on the account and that the documentation was highly supportive to include the code. She called Annette back and informed her of the findings. Annette stated that with the V code, they would not be reimbursed for the encounter. Shondra asked Annette if she could discuss the case with her director when she arrived, which was acceptable.

A few minutes later, Annette called again. This call was about a patient who was being billed for a diagnostic mammogram but did not have a diagnosis code to support medical necessity. Annette asked Shondra whether she could change the code from the screening code to something on the national coverage determination list that would support a diagnostic mammogram. Shondra took down the information, pulled the record, and as far as she could tell, could not find a diagnosis that would support a diagnostic mammogram. Shondra decided to hold this case until Theresa, her director, arrived.

Annette's next call was for a case that Geoffrois had coded. The patient had an arthroscopy of the right knee with a meniscectomy. Geoffrois had assigned two CPT codes, one for the arthroscopic meniscectomy of the knee and one for a diagnostic arthroscopy of the knee. Annette requested that Shondra add modifier 59 so that they would be paid for both procedures. Shondra pulled the record and called Annette back. "This one is easy," she thought to herself. Shondra explained to Annette that she would remove the diagnostic arthroscopy code because that was unbundling in this case. Annette told Shondra that it was their facility policy to always assign the code for the diagnostic procedure if a therapeutic procedure was done and that as long as they assigned modifier 59, it would be reimbursed just fine. Shondra decided again to hold the record until Theresa arrived.

Theresa arrived, and Shondra took all three records in to discuss with her right away. Theresa explained to Shondra that things in the real world are different from what she read about in her textbooks. She told her that general coding guidelines are suggested best practice, but in reality, things need to be done a little differently to maintain the financial well-being and survival of the facility. She explained that modifiers were created for circumstances like this and that it was appropriate to follow Annette's instructions. Shondra insisted that she was uncomfortable with this. Theresa said that it would be fine to leave these calls for Geoffrois's return and that she would handle them for Shondra during Geoffrois's absence.

Shondra remembered the information presented about organization compliance during her orientation. She contacted the internal compliance contact and was directed to Mark Summers, the Chief Financial Officer, who also serves as the Chief Compliance Officer for the facility. Mark, realizing Shondra's lack of experience, provided an explanation similar to that given by Theresa regarding the difference between textbook knowledge and real-life experience. He explained the importance of preserving the bottom line for the organization to survive in a health care world dictated by Medicare reimbursement. Shondra did not feel any better about the situation after her meeting with Mark and doubted not only her decision to work at Springfield General, but also her decision to work as a medical coder.

Discussion Questions

1. How does the American Health Information Management Association Code of Ethics address the situations presented in this case?

2. Are there other "safety nets" for Shondra because the organization's internal reporting system for compliance issues was not effective?

3. What internal and external forces impact Shondra's concerns in this case?

4. What ethical concerns are presented in this case?

5. What legal issues need to be considered regarding this case?

6. Using the case method, evaluate possible actions that Shondra should take and determine the best option.

CASE 28

Legibility and Timeliness Go Hand-in-Hand

Columbus Memorial Hospital is a 200-bed acute care hospital in a city with a population of 125,000. Dr. Ruth Schumann has been a member of active staff at Columbus Memorial Hospital for 23 years. She is a greatly respected surgeon with a spotless record. Her patients rarely have even minor complications after surgery. However, she frequently ends up on the physician suspension list for incomplete records. Dr. Schumann has figured out how to work the system so that she is able to complete just enough of her records to get off of suspension until the next cycle.

Although she prides herself in her perfect record as a surgeon, it is a well-known fact that Dr. Schumann has horribly illegible handwriting. Nursing staff at Columbus Memorial frequently have to contact Dr. Schumann for clarification of orders. Occasionally, they would notice a progress note page added to the patient records for previous dates during patients' hospital stays.

A group of nurses from various units, including the emergency department and surgery, formed a bridge club that plays once a week. One night at bridge, a couple of nurses started discussing Dr. Schumann's documentation practices. Rhonda, who works in surgery, initially listened for a while before she added a comment that gained the attention of the entire group.

Rhonda shared a story about a surgical case of Dr. Schumann's that had a potential complication that did not result in any immediate problems for the patient. She added that she did not think Dr. Schumann had informed the patient or his family about the complication because nothing was overtly wrong at the end of the procedure. The patient had a colon resection, which was basically uncomplicated. However, there was a question regarding the surgical tool count after the patient was closed. Dr. Schumann told the surgical team that she was sure that the count was correct, even though one of the nurses insisted it was not. Rhonda commented to one of the other nurses that it would not surprise her to see the patient readmitted within the next month.

Three weeks later, the patient presented to emergency room (ER) with severe abdominal pain and a high fever. Ladonna, one of the ER nurses on duty when the patient arrived, had been at bridge club the night that Dr. Schumann's documentation was discussed. When the patient's previous records were brought to the emergency department, Ladonna happened to notice that the patient had a colon resection three weeks earlier performed by Dr. Schumann. There was no operative report on the chart, and it was not on the dictation system yet, either. Ladonna pulled the emergency department physician aside and shared Rhonda's story and her concern that this could be the same patient. Radiological exams were completed and demonstrated what appeared to be a solid mass in the patient's abdomen, and the patient was admitted for emergency surgery. Dr. Schumann was out of town, so Dr. O'Malley from the surgical group on call came in to perform the procedure.

Dr. O'Malley entered the patient's abdominal cavity and was amazed to find a clamp that had lacerated a section of the remaining colon, then had become dislodged and punctured another area. Dr. O'Malley successfully repaired the damaged areas, and the patient received five units of packed red blood cells. The patient was taken to the intensive care unit after surgery. It was determined that he had septicemia, and he expired within a week.

The hospital attorneys had already been contacted by the patient's wife's attorney. When the Release of Information Specialist received a request for records from the wife's attorney, he noticed that there still was no operative report from the colon resection, so he had the director contact Dr. Schumann to dictate one as soon as possible.

Dr. Schumann's office gave her a message that stated she needed to dictate an operative report for this patient as soon as possible. However, she was unaware of the pending legal action being taken by the patient's family. She was having an exceptionally busy day because she had just returned from vacation, but she was in no mood to deal with the hospital about incomplete records, so she dictated an operative report based on her documentation at her office.

Not only did the hospital staff have difficulty reading Dr. Schumann's writing, but she occasionally had times when she could not interpret what she had written herself. She read her notes enough to see that the patient had a colon resection, and in the midst of her crazy day, she did not recall the questionable count at the end of the procedure and could not read her own progress note that documented it, so she dictated a completely normal operative note for a colon resection and did not include any documentation about the count. The postoperative orders also included an order for an abdominal x-ray. However, it had not been completed.

Discussion Questions

1. What could potentially happen when this case goes to court?

2. What are the implications of Dr. Schumann's lack of documentation regarding the potential miscount in her dictated operative report?

3. Dr. Schumann wrote a progress note regarding the potential miscount and included an order for an x-ray that was never completed. However, the judge was unable to read Dr. Schumann's writing. Discuss the legal issues related to this situation.

4. Address what could have been done differently by anybody who was aware of the situations in this case.

5. What internal and external forces impact this case?

6. What are the legal issues addressed in this case?

7. What are the ethical issues addressed in this case?

8. How are the ethical issues in this case covered in the American Health Information Management Association Code of Ethics?

9. Using the case method, evaluate possible actions that should be taken and determine the best option.

CASE 29

A Case That Hits Close to Home

Kendra Brown, Registered Health Information Technician, CCS, is the Assistant Director of Health Information Services at Memorial Hospital. Dr. Philip Russell, the chairman of the medical staff committee, enters Kendra's office accompanied by Sue Davidson, the facility risk manager. Sue requests records of all patients in the past two years who have had gastric bypass surgery by Dr. Lester Brown and states that they will be back for them in 20 minutes. Kendra reminds Sue that the department policy for study requests is 24 hours, but Sue tells her that this is an urgent matter. Sue and Kendra are close friends and have both worked at Memorial Hospital for 15 years. Sue confides in Kendra that Dr. Russell needs the records in response to a patient death after surgery, with the family threatening a lawsuit against the facility. She also states that there have been similar incidents with Dr. Brown's patients over the past two years, and Dr. Russell wants to look into the situation and potentially take appropriate action.

Kendra lets Sue know that she will pull the records immediately and thanks her for sharing the information with her. She runs the report of Dr. Brown's patients who have had gastric bypass procedures over the past year and pulls the records from the list. Kendra's mother is scheduled to have gastric bypass surgery by Dr. Brown next week, so naturally, she is curious about the reason for Dr. Russell's inquiry. As Kendra pulls the records for Dr. Russell, she briefly examines the documentation on the charts that indicate a complication may have occurred. She is astonished to discover that all except for one of Dr. Brown's patients were either re-admitted with serious complications or had extended stays due to complications from the procedure. She notes that 24 of the 78 patients expired due to complications from the procedure. Because of these findings, Kendra feels the need to warn her mother to reconsider her decision for surgery or to seek another surgeon.

Kendra returns to her office and calls her mother. Although not revealing any details of her findings, she tells her mother that she has seen something disturbing at work regarding Dr. Brown's gastric bypass patients. She does include her concern regarding the fact that there have been a significant number of gastric bypass patients who have died after the procedure. Kendra asks her mother if she might reconsider her surgery scheduled for next week or at least seek a different surgeon. Sue overhears Kendra's phone conversation and enters Kendra's office. When Kendra gets off the phone, Sue confronts her about the content of her discussion with her mother.

Kendra responds, "I couldn't help but notice a trend in the outcomes of the records I was pulling, especially the number of patients who died after the procedure. Obviously, you are well-aware of what is going on. Wouldn't you do the same thing if your mother were scheduled to have gastric bypass with Dr. Brown?"

Discussion Questions

1. What internal and external forces impact Sue's concerns in this case?

2. What internal and external forces impact Kendra's concerns in this case?

3. What ethical concerns are presented in this case?

4. Discuss the issues presented in this case as they relate to the American Health Information Management Association Code of Ethics.

5. What legal issues need to be considered regarding this case?

6. How should Sue respond to Kendra's statement at the end of this case?

7. List the legal and ethical violations made by Kendra in this case.

8. Discuss the case from both Sue and Kendra's point of view. What would you do if you were in either of their positions?

9. Using the case method, identify what you consider to be the greatest legal or ethical dilemma in this case and determine the best option for resolution.

APPENDIX

American Health Information Management Association Code of Ethics*

Preamble

The ethical obligations of the health information management (HIM) professional include the protection of patient privacy and confidential information; disclosure of information; development, use, and maintenance of health information systems and health records; and the quality of information. Both handwritten and computerized medical records contain many sacred stories—stories that must be protected on behalf of the individual and the aggregate community of persons served in the health care system. Health care consumers are increasingly concerned about the loss of privacy and the inability to control the dissemination of their protected information. Core health information issues include what information should be collected; how the information should be handled, who should have access to the information, and under what conditions the information should be disclosed.

Ethical obligations are central to the professional's responsibility, regardless of the employment site or the method of collection, storage, and security of health information. Sensitive information (genetic, adoption, drug, alcohol, sexual, and behavioral information) requires special attention to prevent misuse. Entrepreneurial roles require expertise in the protection of the information in the world of business and interactions with consumers.

Professional Values

The mission of the HIM profession is based on core professional values developed since the inception of the Association in 1928. These values and the inherent ethical responsibilities for American Health Information Management Association (AHIMA) members and credentialed HIM professionals include providing service, protecting medical, social, and financial information, promoting confidentiality, and preserving and securing health information. Values to the health care team include promoting the quality and advancement of health care, demonstrating HIM expertise and skills, and promoting interdisciplinary cooperation and collaboration. Professional values in relationship to the employer include protecting committee deliberations and complying with laws, regulations, and policies. Professional values related to the public include advocating change, refusing to participate or conceal unethical practices, and reporting violations of practice standards to the proper authorities. Professional values to individual and professional associations include obligations to be honest, bringing honor to self, peers, and profession, committing to continuing education and lifelong learning, performing Association duties honorably, strengthening professional membership, representing the profession to the public, and promoting and participating in research.

These professional values will require a complex process of balancing the many conflicts that can result from competing interests and obligations of those who seek access to health information and require an understanding of ethical decision-making.

Purpose of the American Health Information Management Association Code of Ethics

The HIM professional has an obligation to demonstrate actions that reflect values, ethical principles, and ethical guidelines. The American Health Information Management Association (AHIMA) Code of Ethics sets forth these values and principles to guide conduct. The code is relevant to all AHIMA members and credentialed HIM professionals and students, regardless of their professional functions, the settings in which they work, or the populations they serve.

The AHIMA Code of Ethics serves six purposes:

- Identifies core values on which the HIM mission is based.
- Summarizes broad ethical principles that reflect the profession's core values and establishes a set of ethical principles to be used to guide decision-making and actions.
- Helps HIM professionals identify relevant considerations when professional obligations conflict or ethical uncertainties arise.
- Provides ethical principles by which the general public can hold the HIM professional accountable.
- Socializes practitioners new to the field to HIM's mission, values, and ethical principles.
- Articulates a set of guidelines that the HIM professional can use to assess whether they have engaged in unethical conduct.

The code includes principles and guidelines that are both enforceable and aspirational. The extent to which each principle is enforceable is a matter of professional judgment to be exercised by those responsible for reviewing alleged violations of ethical principles.

The Use of the Code

Violation of principles in this code does not automatically imply legal liability or violation of the law. Such determination can only be made in the context of legal and judicial proceedings. Alleged violations of the code would be subject to a peer review process. Such processes are generally separate from legal or administrative procedures and insulated from legal review or proceedings to allow the profession to counsel and discipline its own members, although in some situations, violations of the code would constitute unlawful conduct subject to legal process.

Guidelines for ethical and unethical behavior are provided in this code. The terms "shall and shall not" are used as a basis for setting high standards for behavior. This does not imply that everyone "shall or shall not" do everything that is listed. For example, not everyone participates in the recruitment or mentoring of students. A HIM professional is not being unethical if this is not part of his or her professional activities; however, if students are part of one's professional responsibilities, there is an ethical obligation to follow the guidelines stated in the code. This concept is true for the entire code. If someone does the stated activities, ethical behavior is the standard. The guidelines are not a comprehensive list. For example, the statement "protect all confidential information to include personal, health, financial, genetic, and outcome information" can also be interpreted as "shall not fail to protect all confidential information to include personal, health, financial, genetic, and outcome information."

A code of ethics cannot guarantee ethical behavior. Moreover, a code of ethics cannot resolve all ethical issues or disputes or capture the richness and complexity involved in striving to make responsible choices within a moral community. Rather, a code of ethics sets forth values and ethical principles and offers ethical guidelines to which professionals aspire and by which their actions can be judged. Ethical behaviors result from a personal commitment to engage in ethical practice.

Professional responsibilities often require an individual to move beyond personal values. For example, an individual might demonstrate behaviors that are based on the values of honesty, providing service to others, or demonstrating loyalty. In addition to these, professional values might require promoting confidentiality, facilitating interdisciplinary collaboration, and refusing to participate in or conceal unethical practices. Professional values could require a more comprehensive set of values than what an individual needs to be an ethical agent in their personal lives.

The AHIMA Code of Ethics is to be used by AHIMA and individuals, agencies, organizations, and bodies (such as licensing and regulatory boards, insurance providers, courts of law, agency boards of directors, government agencies, and other professional groups) that choose to adopt it or use it as a frame of reference. The AHIMA Code of Ethics reflects the commitment of all to uphold the profession's values and to act ethically. Individuals of good character who discern moral questions and, in good faith, seek to make reliable ethical judgments, must apply ethical principles.

The code does not provide a set of rules that prescribe how to act in all situations. Specific applications of the code must take into account the context in which it is being considered and the possibility of conflicts among the code's values, principles, and guidelines. Ethical responsibilities flow from all human relationships, from the personal and familial to the social and professional. Further, the AHIMA Code of Ethics does not specify which values, principles, and guidelines are the most important and ought to outweigh others in instances when they conflict.

Code of Ethics 2004

<u>Ethical Principles:</u> The following ethical principles are based on the core values of the American Health Information Management Association and apply to all HIM professionals.

Health information management professionals:

I. *Advocate, uphold, and defend the individual's right to privacy and the doctrine of confidentiality in the use and disclosure of information.*

II. *Put service and the health and welfare of persons before self-interest and conduct themselves in the practice of the profession so as to bring honor to themselves, their peers, and to the HIM profession.*

III. *Preserve, protect, and secure personal health information in any form or medium and hold in the highest regard the contents of the records and other information of a confidential nature, taking into account the applicable statutes and regulations.*

IV. *Refuse to participate in or conceal unethical practices or procedures.*

V. *Advance HIM knowledge and practice through continuing education, research, publications, and presentations.*

VI. *Recruit and mentor students, peers and colleagues to develop and strengthen professional workforce.*

VII. *Represent the profession accurately to the public.*

VIII. *Perform honorably health information management association responsibilities, either appointed or elected, and preserve the confidentiality of any privileged information made known in any official capacity.*

IX. *State truthfully and accurately their credentials, professional education, and experiences.*

X. *Facilitate interdisciplinary collaboration in situations supporting health information practice.*

XI. *Respect the inherent dignity and worth of every person.*

How to Interpret the Code of Ethics

The following ethical principles are based on the core values of the American Health Information Management Association and apply to all HIM professionals. Guidelines included for each ethical principle are a noninclusive list of behaviors and situations that can help to clarify the principle. They are not to be meant as a comprehensive list of all situations that can occur.

I. *Advocate, uphold, and defend the individual's right to privacy and the doctrine of confidentiality in the use and disclosure of information.*

Health information management professionals shall:

1.1. Protect all confidential information to include personal, health, financial, genetic, and outcome information.

1.2. Engage in social and political action that supports the protection of privacy and confidentiality and be aware of the impact of the political arena on the health information system. Advocate for changes in policy and legislation to ensure protection of privacy and confidentiality, coding compliance, and other issues that surface as advocacy issues as well as facilitating informed participation by the public on these issues.

1.3. Protect the confidentiality of all information obtained in the course of professional service. Disclose only information that is directly relevant or necessary to achieve the purpose of disclosure. Release information only with valid consent from a patient or a person legally authorized to consent on behalf of a patient or as authorized by federal or state regulations. The need-to-know criterion is essential when releasing health information for initial disclosure and all redisclosure activities.

1.4. Promote the obligation to respect privacy by respecting confidential information shared among colleagues, while responding to requests from the legal profession, the media, or other non-health care-related individuals, during presentations or teaching, and in situations that could cause harm to persons.

II. *Put service and the health and welfare of persons before self-interest and conduct themselves in the practice of the profession so as to bring honor to themselves, their peers, and to the health information management profession.*

Health information management professionals shall:

2.1. Act with integrity, behave in a trustworthy manner, elevate service to others above self-interest, and promote high standards of practice in every setting.

2.2. Be aware of the profession's mission, values, and ethical principles, and practice in a manner consistent with them by acting honestly and responsibly.

2.3. Anticipate, clarify, and avoid any conflict of interest, to all parties concerned, when dealing with consumers, consulting with competitors, or in providing services requiring potentially conflicting roles (for example, finding out information about one facility that would help a competitor). The conflicting roles or responsibilities must be clarified, and appropriate action must be taken to minimize any conflict of interest.

2.4. Ensure that the working environment is consistent and encourages compliance with the AHIMA Code of Ethics, taking reasonable steps to eliminate any conditions in their organizations that violate, interfere with, or discourage compliance with the code.

2.5. Take responsibility and credit, including authorship credit, only for work they actually perform or to which they contribute. Honestly acknowledge the work of and the contributions made by others verbally or written, such as in publication.

Health information management professionals **shall not:**

2.6. Permit their private conduct to interfere with their ability to fulfill their professional responsibilities.

2.7. Take unfair advantage of any professional relationship or exploit others to further their personal, religious, political, or business interests.

III. *Preserve, protect, and secure personal health information in any form or medium and hold in the highest regards the contents of the records and other information of a confidential nature obtained in the official capacity, taking into account the applicable statutes and regulations.*

Health information management professionals shall:

3.1. Protect the confidentiality of patients' written and electronic records and other sensitive information. Take reasonable steps to ensure that patients' records are stored in a secure location and that patients' records are not available to others who are not authorized to have access.

3.2. Take precautions to ensure and maintain the confidentiality of information transmitted, transferred, or disposed of in the event of a termination, incapacitation, or death of a health care provider to other parties through the use of any media. Disclosure of identifying information should be avoided whenever possible.

3.3. Inform recipients of the limitations and risks associated with providing services via electronic media (such as computer, telephone, fax, radio, and television).

IV. *Refuse to participate in or conceal unethical practices or procedures.*

Health information management professionals shall:

4.1. Act in a professional and ethical manner at all times.

4.2. Take adequate measures to discourage, prevent, expose, and correct the unethical conduct of colleagues.

4.3. Be knowledgeable about established policies and procedures for handling concerns about colleagues' unethical behavior. These include policies and procedures created by AHIMA, licensing and regulatory bodies, employers, supervisors, agencies, and other professional organizations.

4.4. Seek resolution if there is a belief that a colleague has acted unethically or if there is a belief of incompetence or impairment by discussing their concerns with the colleague when feasible and when such discussion is likely to be productive. Take action through appropriate formal channels, such as contacting an accreditation or regulatory body and/ or the AHIMA Professional Ethics Committee.

4.5. Consult with a colleague when feasible and assist the colleague in taking remedial action when there is direct knowledge of an health information management colleague's incompetence or impairment.

Health information management professionals **shall not:**

4.6. Participate in, condone, or be associated with dishonesty, fraud and abuse, or deception. A noninclusive list of examples includes:

- Allowing patterns of retrospective documentation to avoid suspension or increase reimbursement
- Assigning codes without physician documentation
- Coding when documentation does not justify the procedures that have been billed
- Coding an inappropriate level of service
- Miscoding to avoid conflict with others

- Engaging in negligent coding practices
- Hiding or ignoring review outcomes, such as performance data
- Failing to report licensure status for a physician through the appropriate channels
- Recording inaccurate data for accreditation purposes
- Hiding incomplete medical records
- Allowing inappropriate access to genetic, adoption, or behavioral health information
- Misusing sensitive information about a competitor
- Violating the privacy of individuals

V. *Advance health information management knowledge and practice through continuing education, research, publications, and presentations.*

Health information management professionals shall:

5.1. Develop and enhance continually their professional expertise, knowledge, and skills (including appropriate education, research, training, consultation, and supervision). Contribute to the knowledge base of HIM and share with colleagues their knowledge related to practice, research, and ethics.

5.2. Base practice decisions on recognized knowledge, including empirically based knowledge relevant to health information management and health information management ethics.

5.3. Contribute time and professional expertise to activities that promote respect for the value, integrity, and competence of the health information management profession. These activities may include teaching, research, consultation, service, legislative testimony, presentations in the community, and participation in their professional organizations.

5.4. Engage in evaluation or research that ensures the anonymity or confidentiality of participants and of the data obtained from them by following guidelines developed for the participants in consultation with appropriate institutional review boards. Report evaluation and research findings accurately and take steps to correct any errors later found in published data using standard publication methods.

5.5. Take reasonable steps to provide or arrange for continuing education and staff development, addressing current knowledge and emerging developments related to health information management practice and ethics.

Health information management professionals **shall not:**

5.6. Design or conduct evaluation or research that is in conflict with applicable federal or state laws.

5.7. Participate in, condone, or be associated with fraud or abuse.

VI. *Recruit and mentor students, peers, and colleagues to develop and strengthen professional workforce.*

Health information management professionals shall:

6.1. Evaluate students' performance in a manner that is fair and respectful when functioning as educators or clinical internship supervisors.

6.2. Be responsible for setting clear, appropriate, and culturally sensitive boundaries for students.

6.3. Be a mentor for students, peers, and new health information management professionals to develop and strengthen skills.

6.4. Provide directed practice opportunities for students.

Health information management professionals **shall not:**

6.5. Engage in any relationship with students in which there is a risk of exploitation or potential harm to the student.

VII. *Accurately represent the profession to the public.*

Health information management professionals shall:

7.1. Be an advocate for the profession in all settings and participate in activities that promote and explain the mission, values, and principles of the profession to the public.

VIII. *Perform honorably health information management association responsibilities, either appointed or elected, and preserve the confidentiality of any privileged information made known in any official capacity.*

Health information management professionals shall:

8.1. Perform responsibly all duties as assigned by the professional association.

8.2. Resign from an Association position if unable to perform the assigned responsibilities with competence.

8.3. Speak on behalf of professional health information management organizations, accurately representing the official and authorized positions of the organizations.

IX. *State truthfully and accurately their credentials, professional education, and experiences.*

Health information management professionals shall:

9.1. Make clear distinctions between statements made and actions engaged in as a private individual and as a representative of the health information management profession, a professional health information organization, or the health information management professional's employer.

9.2. Claim and ensure that their representations to patients, agencies, and the public of professional qualifications, credentials, education, competence, affiliations, services provided, training, certification, consultation received, supervised experience, and other relevant professional experience are accurate.

9.3. Claim only those relevant professional credentials actually possessed and correct any inaccuracies occurring regarding credentials.

X. *Facilitate interdisciplinary collaboration in situations supporting health information practice.*

Health information management professionals **shall:**

10.1. Participate in and contribute to decisions that affect the well-being of patients by drawing on the perspectives, values, and experiences of those involved in decisions related to patients. Professional and ethical obligations of the interdisciplinary team as a whole and of its individual members should be clearly established.

XI. *Respect the inherent dignity and worth of every person.*

Health information management professionals shall:

11.1. Treat each person in a respectful fashion, being mindful of individual differences and cultural and ethnic diversity.

11.2. Promote the value of self-determination for each individual.

Acknowledgment

Adapted with permission from the Code of Ethics of the National Association of Social Workers.

Resources

AHIMA Code of Ethics, 1957, 1977, 1988, and 1998.

Harman, L.B., ed. *Ethical Challenges in the Management of Health Information.* Gaithersburg, MD: Aspen, 2001.

National Association of Social Workers. "Code of Ethics." http://www.naswdc.org (accessed 1999).

Revised and adopted by AHIMA House of Delegates – July 1, 2004

Index